DANIEL AND
"THE TIME OF THE END"

Has the Seal Been Broken?

By: Gerald L. "Gary" Fix

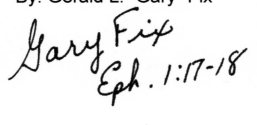

Gary Fix
Eph. 1:17-18

CONTENTS

PREFACE...vii

THEOLOGICAL THEORIZING 13
PERSPECTIVE ON HERMENEUTICS:
    BIBLICAL INTERPRETATION................. 32
THE ORACLE.. 54
NEBUCHADNEZZAR'S DREAM AND
    DANIEL'S VISION 79

ADENDUM or EPILOG –
    HOW I CAME TO WRITE THIS
    PAPER 145

DANIEL AND
"THE TIME OF THE END"

PREFACE

B efore reading this document it is important to understand that it is not intended
as a paper of great scholarly work, nor as an
authoritative rendering of academic excellence.
Any who know me at all know that I am no great
scholar! I am quite sure it would be possible to
make this into a more scholarly document, but
as Solomon very wisely and truly stated, "...*of
making of many books there is no end*", (Eccl.
12:12). I am not at all convinced of the wisdom of
contributing to this 'endless' venture. Nor would
I pretend that my own limited scholarship on any
of these matters would match, let alone surpass,
the scholarship of others who have already

written or may yet write. However, I do believe the Lord has granted some new insight and understanding on this subject by means other than pure scholarship or academics. These insights are at least worthy of close scrutiny by those who would be more scholarly. We are told in the pages of the book that these prophecies of Daniel were "sealed" by God "...***until the time of the end***..."! (Dan. 12:4&9). Well, the "...***until the time of the end***..." has now come and the seal, therefore, is to be broken according to this prophecy. When Daniel read in the writings of Jeremiah that the people of Israel would be in captivity for seventy years, he did not run immediately to pack up all of his things, only to sit down and wait for someone to get things moving and start the trek back home. Instead, he fell on his face before God and began to plead with Him with great urgency and fervency to fulfill His Word. He confessed the sins of his people, and begged God's forgiveness, while engaging in "... *prayer and supplications, with fasting, sackcloth,* *and ashes.*" He presented his appeal to the Lord eloquently and fervently until God brought His Word to fulfillment. Even so, prayer has been offered similar to Daniel that God would break the seal and give insight into all that has been shut up and sealed for these 2500 years, plus.

It now seems evident that insights into this prophecy have been obtained by means that will be explained in this book. Much prayer over a rather long period of time was offered up, and when the insights came, it was most surprising and rather sudden! But for now we will simply present this with the sincere prayer that every heart that is truly able to receive the things of the Spirit of God will, by the means described here, recognize Truth and error. I genuinely welcome any and all comments, favorable or otherwise, whether in agreement or disagreement. I urge all who read this to do so with Bible and con-cordance close at hand, and to "*...search the Scriptures daily to see if these things are so.*" In the final analysis, His Word is the final authority,

ix

and any new insights are subject to, and must always comply with the Word, impeccably! I pray that the Spirit of God, Who is the Spirit of Truth Whom Jesus promised would *"...teach you all things"*, and would *"...lead you into all Truth"* will perform this work for us all in this matter.

This topic, prophecy concerning the end times, has become very popular among church people and secular people alike. Many books treat this subject with great flair and drama, and maybe some sensationalism. The growing abundance of these books, particularly those by Hal Lindsey, has helped stimulate this popular interest. Many of these books have found their way into the secular market, and are being purchased in large numbers. It is not at all improper that this interest should be increasing, seeing that so many of the events foretold by the prophets and the apostles, and by Christ Himself, are unfolding right before our eyes! Anybody who has even a meager understanding of Scripture can see the increase of earthquakes, famines, droughts, extremes of destructive weather, the return of Jews to the land of their heritage, the unfolding of the events involving the peoples from "*...the regions of the north...*", (Russia, etc.), and numerous other plain prophetic statements relative to the final hours of time. The nations identified in Ezekiel 38 and 39 are coming together like never before in history, and are already allies in their hatred for Israel, intent on their destruction, just as Ezekiel prophesied 2500 years ago!

Before making our examination of the actual prophecies of Daniel, we need to address a couple of other matters in laying a foundation for the presentation. Some contemporary approaches to the Word need to be carefully examined in the light of Scripture, itself, as well as in the light of the means or methods of the men of God throughout the centuries of Christianity in determining their understandings of the Word. Please be patient as you read these things in preparation for seeing what Daniels prophecies have to say.

THEOLOGICAL THEORIZING

In our culture and society we have fallen in love with the idea of "theorizing." The scientific method has pervaded virtually all of our learning processes, and there are no areas of thinking which have not been affected by this approach. In many areas of academic discipline the theoretical process is virtually unavoidable, and is actually preferable, because of the dearth or absence of sufficient proofs. Therefore it becomes necessary to theorize, and from there to pursue studies based on the best existing theories.

In no place is this more evident, at least in the public perception, than in the field of Biology

or Life Sciences. In the prideful human reasoning of recent generations, man decided that
the "simple-minded" declarations of the religious
reliance on the teachings of the Bible were just
plain nonsense to their way of thinking. So the
human mind had to begin to gather up all the
physical evidence that could be found, no matter
how minimal, and devise or conjure up some kind
of workable "hypothesis" from which to operate.
Hence, the famous (or infamous) "*theory* of evolution". The tiniest bits and pieces of evidence
are expanded and built upon by very imaginative minds to put together a proposed plausible
picture to suggest where things came from,
and their origin. Consequently, man began to
rely upon his own inventive, imaginative mental
abilities, honed and sharpened by his own very
finite whetstone, to attempt to extract supposed
'truth' from very minimal evidence. You and I
believe that this has not only failed, but has, in
fact, failed *miserably*! But the effect has been to
bring man to a place of unjustifiable pride. He

has become so pleased with himself and deeply in love with his own perceived and imagined reasoning abilities that he has become virtually unapproachable by anything of legitimate Truth. Solomon totally and properly declared in Proverbs that only a fool would dare say in his heart that there is no God!

Something that is so sad in all of this is that we in the Christian community have succumbed to the very same kind of philosophy, and have adopted methods of approach to our Biblical and theological learning that God never intended for us! We have apparently become reliant upon our own natural, carnal thinking ability rather than on any true and genuine revelation or enlightenment of the Spirit of God, the One Jesus called the "Spirit of Truth". As a result, we have begun to "...*walk in the counsel of the ungodly...*" by ever so gradually adopting their methods and approach to learning. It is not even proper to speak of the biblical teaching of beginnings as the "creation *theory*". The

15

generally accepted definition of theory makes this totally improper! A theory is defined as a conclusion based on existing evidence which is incomplete. Compiling bits and pieces of evidence and aligning them in a kind of logical sequence which leads to a tentative conclusion is what we call a "theory". (A theory is <u>always</u> a tentative conclusion that lasts only until it is either refuted, or further evidence is obtained causing the conclusion to either be affirmed or changed. This is *constantly* happening with the theory of evolution!) By that definition, the creation account as presented in the Bible is not even close to being a theory. Some may wish to call it a "myth", or a "legend" if they so choose. But it can in no way be called a theory. It is <u>not</u> a conclusion based on the compiling of evidence of any kind. It is, in reality, a statement or declaration recorded by Moses, as we believe from the direct revelation and inspiration of God, and that is <u>not</u>, by anybody's definition, a theory.

16

The same thing can and must be said about any approach to any of the teachings or doctrines of the Bible. The Scriptures, themselves, speak *only* of the principle of "Truth and error". Whatever we believe about what the Bible says is either Truth or error. As I will continue to point out at various places throughout this book, we are not going to be judged by God according to what we *thought* the Bible said, but by what it *actually* says. It is extremely important, then, is it not, that we make absolutely certain we have it straight, not just that we have the best theory. There is no place given in any of the teachings of Scripture for Theological Theorizing or anything akin to it. And yet for so many years it appears that we have become accustomed to doing just exactly that.

There are many possible examples that could be given to illustrate this practice. All the variations on the doctrine of water baptism is one such example. There are multiple variations on the degree of its importance to salvation, on

17

the modes or practices, and any other ramifica-
tions surrounding it. As with any other teaching
of the Bible, God does not grant the privilege of
choosing our own favorite theory, and doing it
any which way we please, while expecting God
to honor our own personal interpretation. Any
theory is either Truth, or it is error in the sight
of God, and He grants us literally all the assistance we need to determine what the truth is
with certainty.

The things which we will be covering in
this book are matters about which many have
written and taught over the years, and have
approached from many different angles, coming
to several different conclusions. It should be as
obvious, in this, as well as in any other issue of
the Word, that there can only be *one* legitimate
"**TRUTH**"! *All* teachings must necessarily come
under the heading of 'error' except that one to
which God, Himself, attests, and He has made it
clear that He will do just that for *all* who "…*wills
to do the will of the Father…*" (John 7:17)

18

John Wesley is acknowledged to have been an outstanding man of God, and he made reference to this principle in one of his more notable sermons, in which he spoke in rather strong language against many of the ministers of his day for this very practice. He stated that they would set about to preach the thoughts or imaginations of their own minds, even often attributing these thoughts to the Spirit of God. And yet, as he stated, they were masterfully mingling truth and error, and nobody seemed able to discern between the one and the other. He called such theorizers "false prophets"! (From "The Standard Sermons of John Wesley" vol. II).

The influence of this kind of thinking brings with it a serious diminishing of the deep respect and reverence for the sacredness of Truth, which God expects us to have. We begin to view the legitimate Truth of God as something to be toyed with so as to be able to come up with something new and intriguing to the intellect, which the Scripture states amounts to being "...*carried* about by every wind of doctrine..." (Eph. 4:14) and "...ever learning, but never able to come to knowledge of the Truth..." (II Tim. 3:7) and "...having itching ears..." (II Tim. 4:3). In another place it speaks of "...vain imaginings and foolish speculations..." (Romans 1:21 – AMP) Christian Doctrine becomes too much like human philosophy, which can be adjusted and modified from time to time to suit particular fickle whims and tastes. So it becomes also with theorizing. This is the very thing which got the Scribes and Pharisees into rather serious trouble, though it wasn't called by this name. This is also the very kind of thing the Prophet Isaiah was talking about in Is. 65:2, where he writes, "*I have spread out My hands all day long to a rebellious people, who walk in the way which is not good, <u>following their own thoughts</u>.*" There is a very real sense in which, in our theorizing or seeking to find in our own inventiveness the sense of Truth which God presents, we are being "...*a rebellious people*...", just as Isaiah says.

20

Getting saved, or even being filled with the Holy Spirit of God, is no sure guarantee in itself that our thoughts then are always from God. Virtually everybody knows this. However, as stated elsewhere, each Theological Theorist will proclaim long and loud that his particular theory or doctrine has been taught to him by the Holy Spirit. A truly objective observer can readily see the absurdity of this! It is still all too obvious that the Holy Spirit *cannot possibly* be so devious as to teach one man one thing, then turn around and teach another man something completely contradictory. It seems that somebody, or *many somebodies*' are contriving theories and/or philosophies, then attributing them to the Holy Spirit, teaching something which can't be anything but error, and blaming God for it. I am quite certain that this is certainly not their intent, and they may all very well be sincere in their attitudes. But it is also quite obviously possible to be "sincerely wrong". What appears to have happened is that we have departed from the

21

seriousness of the necessity of determining the principle of "Truth and error," and lost the sense of the sacredness and holiness of God's Truth. We have left off our utter dependence upon the New Testament "Oracle", and have turned for our dependence to our own human thoughts and reasoning ability. The Real Truth is no longer viewed as sacred. It has become, as stated before, a matter of philosophizing and adopting our own "private interpretation." The principle expressed in I Corinthians 1:10 has little or no meaning to us any more. We are unavoidably left with the conclusion that God has placed in our hands "*...the sum of [His] Word...*" which is "*...infinite Truth,*" filled with enigmas and mysteries and hard sayings, and then left it to us to figure it all out with just our own very limited, finite minds as the only tool at our disposal. This is tantamount to accusing God, wrongfully, of toying with us.

With all the various shades of doctrine which have permeated the church, we also are left unavoidably to conclude that the Spirit of Truth has led us, the Church, into all confusion instead of "all Truth". The Word admonishes us in many places and in many ways to "*...lean not to your own understanding...*", (Prov. 3:5) and yet we insist on maintaining our privilege of doing just that when it comes to matters of doctrine or Theology, as though God would not assist us and provide us with the necessary revelation or illumination which He has promised, to help prevent us from buying into error.

This theorizing has also had the effect of softening our hatred of error. Oh, we still despise the errors of the cults and of anything which contradicts our convictions on the principles of salvation, or on the nature of God. But when we take to ourselves the privilege of theorizing, or "private interpretation" on this teaching of the Word, we diminish any sense of caution toward the problem of error. We have forsaken the understanding that error is nothing if it is not a refuting of the Truth, hence a *lie*! It is so much more than

23

merely a simple, honest mistaken opinion, as we have been led to believe. No matter how minimal it may seem to us, a lie is a lie, and it has only one source according to Christ Himself. He identifies for us the one whom He calls, "...*the Father of lies!*" (John 8:44) When we are careless enough to think, in our human pride, that we can read and figure out for ourselves by the use of our finite mental powers any part of that which is "infinite Truth", we become susceptible and fall prey to the deceiver even to just that small, seemingly insignificant extent.

Paul stated very clearly that "*The natural man receiveth not the things of the Spirit of God, for they are foolishness to him. Neither can he know them, for they are [only] spiritually discerned*". (I Corinthians 2:14). Maybe we have become much too casual toward "carnality", not realizing or acknowledging that this leads to the inability to receive the things of the Spirit of God, which includes His ministry of teaching all things, and leading into all Truth, which Christ

24

told us He would do. The fact that the things of the Spirit are *only* spiritually discerned makes it obvious that we, in fact, <u>can</u> discern Truth and error by means of the Holy Spirit, when we are in the mode of willing to "do the will of the Father...", as Jesus said, *"He who wills to do the will of the Father **shall know** of the doctrine [teaching] whether it be of God or whether I speak of myself,"* (John 7:17).

The quantity of the variations on doctrine and Theology within the current church would certainly seem to imply that there certainly must be many who have been living carnal lives, and in various aspects of their lives have apparently been unwilling to do the will of the Father, while still presuming to write and teach things of doctrine and Theology, would it not? If we have been left a promise by Jesus that we can be led into all Truth, and can be taught all things by the Spirit of God, but that our ability to actually "know" or recognize Truth is closely tied to our willingness to do the will of the Father, then

25

would it not be very reasonable to conclude that we must needs be very careful to walk consistently in the Spirit, according to the will of the Father if we are to expect to maintain any hope whatsoever of being and remaining in "The Truth" or being preserved from error?

Much of what has been said here is verified and enlarged upon in the writings of Jesse Penn-Lewis, the writer from the early part of the twentieth century who penned the teachings of one of the truly great men of God of this age, or *any* age, Evan Roberts. These two were deeply concerned, and quite properly so, over the degree of deception and error which had crept into the established church, causing a great diminishing of the manifestation of the power of God. They spoke and wrote concerning the things which brought about the deceptions and errors which people were prone to fall for, and ways and means provided by God through His Word for defending against these deceptions. Rather than elaborating further on the subject, if this

26

has stirred your interest even a little bit, it would be well worth your while to examine this book, "War On the Saints", by Jesse Penn-Lewis. For any who have a real love for the Truth as a principle in their hearts, this will help immensely in efforts to discern between Truth and error, and will aid in determining if there is any valid, legitimate truth to the things contained in this book.

Yes!! It really *is* possible to remain free from error and assured of the Truth. The Apostle John did not write in vain, *"We are from God: He who knows God listens to us: He who is not from God does not listen to us. **By this we know the Spirit of Truth and the spirit of error!"** (I John 4:6).

Theorizing just simply does not get it in any legitimate quest for Truth! There are very obviously many things in the Word that are to be understood *only* as the Spirit gives that understanding. There is, in fact, only one thing in the Word which we are told is not ours to know. That fact strongly implies that all other things

27

<u>are</u> for our knowledge and understanding, and are <u>not</u> for guesswork or speculation, or *theorizing*. If we, with patience and perseverance pursue with all genuine humility to find out what God has to say on a subject, He will not by any means violate His promises, and He *will* give both the knowledge and the understanding which we desire of Him. It may not come all at once - in fact, it probably won't - but *it will come*! If we are careful and diligent to actually walk in all the truth we already have, and strive with all the same care and diligence to "*...do the will of the Father...*", and maintain a close and intimate relationship with His Holy Spirit, resisting the temptations to speculate and theorize, we can be assured of being kept free from error and deception, and of being led by Him into all Truth, just as Jesus promised.

No - with The WORD

In the light of all this, now it is time to consider for a few moments a matter of seemingly relative obscurity on the subject at hand. If we are going to see the prophecies of Daniel in their

28

full light, this is a principle that we must examine carefully. It seems that very little attention has been given to the fact that the prophecies concerning the first coming of the Messiah were very clear and specific and explicit. The prophecies of this event even gave a clear declaration of the precise timing of His appearance. Daniel foretold, and not in a mystery or parable, that the time of the Messiah's appearance on the scene would be 483 years following the issuing of the command to rebuild Jerusalem (Dan.9:25). That prophetic timing was so precise that the Bible scholars and religious leaders of the Jews of that day were actually expecting Him to appear at the very time Jesus came on the scene. These lawyers and scribes and priests, whether of the sect of the Pharisees or Sadducees, or of some other, were very well versed in the prophetic statements of the Scriptures concerning this. They quoted for Herod the prophecy concerning His birthplace without having to look it up, or make a search for it. Old Simeon knew

29

that the time was right and that he would not depart this world until he had *"seen the Lord's Christ"* (Lk.2:25-35). The elderly prophetess, Anna, also anticipated His coming at that very time, and actually recognized Him when He was a mere infant of eight days (vss.36-38). The fact of His coming and the certainty of the time of His arrival was no mystery at all to any of the biblical scholars of the day, *yet virtually all of them failed utterly to recognize Him for Who He really was!*

In all of their intellectualizing on the whole matter, they found it impossible for their minds to correlate a Messiah described as "despised and rejected", "afflicted", "suffering", etc., with a Messiah "conquering", "ruling", "delivering", "reigning on the throne of David". So they felt they had to choose between the two apparently conflicting descriptions which prophesied a Messiah for Whom they were looking. They chose to look for the latter one. They chose in their intellectualizing and theorizing to ignore the things they could not understand or fit into

30

the picture they wanted to see. Something was terribly wrong with their understanding and interpretation of the Scripture - the "academics"! Jesus, Himself, told them that they had "... *eyes but see not, and ears, but hear not...*" Just as Isaiah had depicted them many centuries before, (Mark 8:18). Keep reading and you will see how this fits the current status of the church.

A PERSPECTIVE ON HERMENEUTICS: BIBLICAL INTERPRETATION

I had the great privilege of teaching a class in the South Pacific Bible College in Fiji on Hermeneutics. I believe it would be totally appropriate and beneficial here to insert some thoughts and observations on the principle of Biblical Interpretation, or "Hermeneutics". God has, indeed, provided a way for us to read and interpret His Word correctly, and we need to know just what He has provided and made available to us for that purpose!

*"But know this first of all, that **no prophecy of Scripture is a matter of one's own [private]***

interpretation, *for no prophecy was ever made by an act of human will, but men moved by the Holy Spirit spoke from God", (I Peter 1:20).* NO NEW REVELATION AD 96

This statement of Scripture has caused some difficulties among some Bible scholars, as well as among some of us simple believers in the church. Virtually *everyone* wants to pre-serve for themselves the privilege of personal, private interpreting of the things they read in the Scripture. Virtually *all* of us want to be able to say, "As I read it, this is what I think it means." The obvious problem with this is that so many different people read it in so many different ways. Consequently, we see the results of this attitude in such a tremendously wide variations of believings about virtually every subject in the Bible throughout the entire realm of Christianity. There is such an explosion of different doctrines and so many variations of Theology that we are unable to give people in the world, or even in the church for that matter, any confidence at all in the principle of Truth in the Christian community.

33

We have become adversaries within the ranks, arguing and debating with each other, vying for the privilege of presenting our own particular variation of the truth to any who will listen or be persuaded. These differences have spawned an incredible number of fights and arguments and splits and contentions, and tremendous confusion, over the centuries of Christianity, and all because people are so much inclined to either ignore or overlook, or simply just not understand, the principle being stated here in this statement of the Apostle Peter, who is writing under the direct inspiration of the Holy Spirit of God.

The Apostle Paul touches on the same principle when he writes in I Corinthians 1:10 (Amp.), "*But I urge and entreat you, brethren, by the name of the Lord Jesus Christ, that all of you be in <u>perfect harmony</u>, and in <u>full agreement</u> in what you say, and that there be <u>no dissensions or factions or divisions among you</u>; but that you be <u>perfectly united</u> in your common understanding <u>**and** in your opinions and judgments.</u>*" Just a simple, though careful, reading of that Spirit-inspired statement makes it clear, first of all, that God does not desire or intend that we *ever* be in disagreement on <u>*anything*</u>, let alone on the things He has to say in His Word! And secondly, it becomes obvious that it is actually possible to be like this, else He would never have made this strongly worded statement through his holy Apostle, Paul. We must acknowledge, however, that it is definitely **not** possible to accomplish this in our own human abilities. If it is to be accomplished, and if this Scripture is ever to be fulfilled, it has to be done according to a means which the Scripture prescribes.

The science or study of biblical interpreta-tion, or "Hermeneutics," is actually an inexact science at best, as has been so commonly demonstrated. The goal is to produce an objective examination of the Scriptures and draw valid conclusions on any particular subject or passage by this means. This objectivity which is essential in this approach is not even possible because of the obvious character and nature of our humanness. Interpretive analysis of Scripture whether we like to admit it or not, is inevitably tainted by our own individual prejudices and preconceived ideas. It is also going to be tainted by our seriously limited understanding of spiritual things in our human senses. When we study Hermeneutics from the perspective of someone with a strong Calvinistic bias or prejudice, we would be led to understand or interpret the Scripture in a particular biased manner. Studying the same subject or passage from the perspective of a strong Wesleyan/Arminian persuasion or prejudice, a very different conclusion would be reached using the same principles of hermeneutics, showing the "science" to be inexact. The matter is further complicated if it were to be studied from a scholarly Pentecostal instructor, bringing us to a different conclusion yet. This can only cause the issue to be all the more confusing and complex, which is certainly not godly.

It is quite obviously impossible to base any interpretation of Scripture on a completely objective and unbiased approach, humanly speaking, no matter how sincerely we try. We inevitably end up interpreting whatever we read or study in the light of our own personal experience or prior understanding. We just can't help but appeal to our own experience, or to the experience of *SUBJECTIVE* others we know or are aware of, to illustrate or verify our particular interpretation of the Word. Yet this science admonishes us that personal experience, or human experience is no sound basis for determining or establishing doctrine. The Word *YES* of God **alone**, they say, must be the sole basis for determining sound doctrine. But because so many have been led to believe somehow that God's Word is subject to their own individual pri- *Beware* vate interpretation, we have observed through the centuries the development of a confusing conglomerate of doctrines and beliefs within the church in clear violation and contradiction of I Cor.1:10. Interpretation of Scripture **has become**

37

a private matter, which is totally contrary to the very clear admonition of the Word.

As for the part personal experience plays, the Apostle Paul himself is a perfect example of the necessity of 'experience' in understanding the Word. As Saul of Tarsus, a Jew and a "Pharisee of the Pharisees," he had a very thorough and meticulous knowledge of the Scriptures, and a very solid foundation of doctrine and theology. He was highly educated, well-credentialed and highly qualified as an interpreter of the Jewish Scripture. But when he had that 'experience' with Jesus on the road to Damascus, he did not go and search the Scriptures to see if the experience was valid according to the prevailing 'sound doctrine' of his day and his sect. Just the opposite occurred. He searched the Scriptures *in the light of* that new experience, and as a consequence his theology was modified and his believing was transformed. It becomes the height of pride or arrogance, not to mention folly, to hold to a theological position or believing in

38

the light of the overwhelming evidence to the contrary of this kind of experience. O, God! Deliver us all from such pride and arrogance!

Peter also, who penned the words we are now examining, was well established in his doctrine and theology, and had been filled with the Holy Spirit, walking in the Spirit for a while when he had a personal experience which altered his doctrine for all time (Acts 10:9-16). He would **never** eat anything unclean or profane. His theology was already determined, and would never permit such a thing. Yet in his "experience", his believing and doctrine changed as he was instructed by God, completely contrary to his understanding of the Word, to *"kill and eat!"*

As mentioned, we are taught to resist using experience as a means of determining, or helping to determine, sound doctrine. Experience is undependable and fickle, and it cannot be relied upon for such an important matter. However, those who do so strongly advocate this inevitably cite their own 'experience' of salvation as substantiating proof of the validity of the doctrine, and very properly so. In order to have a full understanding of the doctrine of salvation, it must necessarily be experienced! The doctrine of the Baptism of the Holy Spirit is another prime example. There is such a tremendous amount of disagreement, and variation of opinions, on the subject among theologians today, but virtually **all** who eventually enter into the actual experience, even those who had formerly been opposed on theological grounds, testify that they quite suddenly had their spiritual eyes opened, and they now understand the actual doctrine for the very first time. Legitimate experience *must*, of necessity, play a major role in the ability to understand doctrine. I have often thought of sitting under the teaching of some man who teaches about prayer, but I would feel much more confident learning from someone who has experienced the kinds of things in prayer that are written about John Hyde or George Mueller rather than a mere scholar who has made a thorough study of the subject

40

with nothing to show in the way of experience for his great knowledge and expertise.

I have longed to have a good and thorough understanding of the subject of what we call "revival," which amounts to the moving and working of the Spirit of God in His Church, resulting in powerful conviction of sin and the bringing of people to a place of genuine repentance. But I want to sit at the feet of a man who has actually experienced it, rather than a man who has made even a lifetime study of the principles but has never had the experience of making those principles actually work! Genuine understanding of **any** of the working doctrines or principles of the Word can never be obtained apart from **experiencing** those working principles.

Is it improper to say that we have become a sorry lot when we have to resort to the use of a demonstrably inexact, man-made science as a basis for our beliefs? This approach to interpreting Scripture is itself insupportable by the very Word of God it purports to interpret. In other

41

words, it is unscriptural! The first two chapters of I Corinthians refute **any** human attempt to examine Truth with any hope of coming to valid conclusions. This Word of God, in order for it to have *any* degree of validity to *any* individual, *must be taught by the Holy Ghost.* Then, and **only then**, can it be said to be *"of no private interpretation."* Even when Jesus was teaching His disciples, and He asked them who men were saying that He was, and they answered Him with many obviously speculative wrong answers, He taught them this very principle. When He then turned the question to them more personally, Peter's response in speaking for the whole group was not based on any scholarship of a higher order, or even necessarily comparable to those whom they had just quoted; nor was it based on any superior methodology of interpretation which they had devised. That response was based solely and entirely on direct revelation from God, and was attested so by Christ Himself: *"And Jesus answered and said unto him, Blessed art*

42

thou, Simon Barjona: for flesh and blood hath not revealed it unto thee, but my Father which is in heaven." (Matt. 16:17)

It remains completely inconceivable that "*My Father which is in heaven*" would provide that revelation for Peter and by inference the rest of the disciples, and would then give a different revelation to someone else. But that is precisely what we are led to believe by the use of and dependence on the traditional principles of hermeneutics! And this is precisely what we see as the result. It cannot help but be faulty and produce these kinds of results because it must rely on the human ability to acquire and correlate information sufficiently, completely and accurately to be able to arrive at a valid conclusion. Such reliance on human ability and human wisdom can only produce much confusion and disagreement, resulting in unholy, ungodly fights, splits, contentions and dissension and strife, which in fact it has done!

43

The results of all this is that we who are of limited education, or are just plain uneducated on any of these matters, despair of ever being able to get a handle on truth. We are left with the unenviable task or responsibility of hearing various interpretations from outstanding scholars, and with our limited resources must choose which scholarly authority to accept. The scholastic accomplishments or intellectual abilities of these men seem to have little or no significance, because we find ourselves in the position of disagreement with many men of out-standing intellectual and academic credentials.

There are many more examples which could be presented. We could examine the differences between John Calvin's five points of the "TULIP" (**T**otal Depravity, **U**nconditional Predestination/Election, **L**imited Atonement, **I**rresistible Grace, and final **P**erseverance of the Saints), and James Arminius' point by point presentation of the principles of man's complete freedom of will. These points are not a matter of opinion! God's Truth on this subject is *"forever settled in heaven"* (Psalm 119:89) and is not subject to any man's interpretation. It is **NOT** a matter of which man is right! It is solely a matter of "what saith the Lord!!" It is not even possible that both are right, but it is possible that both could be wrong! Only the "Spirit of Truth" can discern this for us. This is by no means to demean the quality of either of these men, or their legitimate claim to salvation "*...by grace... through faith"*. It is only a clear picture of the vanity of using our unaided and finite human intellect to attempt to come to the knowledge of God's infinite Truth. It just simply cannot be done. Even the regenerated mind is still quite finite, but God's Word and Truth are infinite. The finite can only receive the infinite by means of revelation and illumination from the Infinite Source of the infinite knowledge. When will man ever learn? When will the proper humility in acknowledging and placing our utter and complete dependence on the promised ministry and work of the Holy Spirit ever bring Christians to the point of abandoning something which is so demonstrably unscriptural and undependable, and so fraught with pride? The Spirit of revelation and illumination is still an absolute essential, and is still available! (Eph. 1:17)

NO!
Rev. 22:18
Deut 4:2,
12:32

It is important to note that the disciples themselves, even after spending some three and a half years under the greatest teacher this world has ever seen, the very One who was *"the Word … made flesh,"* at the end of His earthly ministry and just moments before His ascension, they still needed Him to *"open their understanding that they might <u>understand</u> the Scriptures"* (Lk.24:45). If **they** needed that kind of help from the Lord after the intensive teaching they had received, *how much more do we?* It might also be argued, and with some degree of validity, that many throughout the years of the church who professed to have the Holy Ghost, have been just as diverse in their doctrines. And even today there are many men of all theological persuasions who make claims to have had the illumination

46

and inspiration of the Holy Spirit. The fact is that virtually all who teach the Scriptures make such claims, and many may sincerely believe it! I haven't yet heard anyone who was willing to say that the Spirit of God didn't have anything to do with their understanding of the Word. Just because someone actually may have been filled with the Holy Spirit does not guarantee that they will always avail themselves of any one part of His work or ministry. The promise Jesus gave was a promise of the availability of the Spirit's ministry, and this work was granted as a *provision* for any who were thus filled, and who would avail themselves of that provision. Any provision is only accessed by faith and is never to be considered automatic. Such a wide range of differences of opinion make it abundantly clear, sadly, that many are mistaken in their believing.

What remains then for us is that we 1) seek diligently to be filled with the Spirit; 2) seek on a consistent, daily basis to walk in and be led by the Spirit in all things; 3) learn to practice calling

47

and stay in the written completed word!

on Him and depending upon Him to fulfill His promise to lead **you**, personally, into all Truth, and teach **you** all things, learning to access by faith the means available for testing the Truth and trying the spirits; 4) get humble, and acknowledge our utter and complete dependence upon Him! Then, and only then, can we be assured and have confidence that we actually know and recognize the Truth when we hear it or read it.

We must always keep in mind that the Word itself makes it very clear that we will have no excuse when we stand before God for holding to anything that is error, or a lie. He has provided for us a perfectly valid means of obtaining from Him an understanding of the Truth and preservation from error. If we fail or neglect to avail ourselves of that which He has provided, we stand without excuse. If we maintain our 'right' in utterly despicable pride to interpret what He says on our own, we stand without excuse!! John the Beloved's first Epistle is literally full of statements which assert that **we can know** the

48

Truth, and can actually discern between Truth and error. It matters not that many thousands may have failed or neglected to avail themselves of these promises, provisions and admonitions; it only remains that we **do**! The Truth which God has made available to us can and will *never* be seen or understood unless and until we do.

Still one more thought before we proceed further with the prophecies of Daniel. It has been argued by some that there are certain points of doctrine which are basic and essential, and are therefore to be treated with much more caution or care, while other parts of Scripture which are deemed "non-essential" may be handled with *what?* more flexibility in interpretation. What has yet to be answered, however, is what teachings fall into which category, and by what standard or criteria is that determined.

On what basis can we determine and declare *anything* from the Word to be "non-essential?" We could also ask, by what or whose authority are the categories of essential and non-essential established? The Word of God itself does not declare *any* issue within its content to be unimportant or non-essential! Any such determination becomes arbitrary on the part of any particular viewpoint. Any teaching or portion of Scripture which was considered by God to be sufficiently important to include in the sacred writings, to present to us as "God-breathed," should be considered sacred enough by us to make absolutely certain we get it straight, have it straight, and teach it straight. We are told that *"ALL Scripture is inspired of God..."* (God-breathed) (II Tim. 3:16). How can we ever justify in our thinking the declaring of any portion of it unimportant or 'non-essential'? We **must** take care that we not play games with interpreting or theorizing on that which is sacred and holy, when we could and should be seeking God with a humble and earnest heart for revelation and illumination that like those original disciples **our** understandings also might be opened by Him, so that we, too, might understand the Scriptures.

50

Jesus taught that *"... if any man wills to do His will, he <u>shall **know** of the doctrine</u>* (teaching), *whether it be of God or whether I speak of Myself."* (John 7:17) It appears quite certain that **before** we ever make efforts to know or understand the Word of Truth, we must take care that we honestly and earnestly and diligently seek to *"...do the will of the Father,"* no matter what that will proves to be, or where it proves to lead us. We could very well be guilty of trying to figure out or take personal control of our own destiny, making all the plans and preparations for our lives, then assuming that God will step in and bless us in it all, rather than making diligent effort to know, before making our plans, just what He has in store for us and wants us to do. Failing to even seek to know His will, yet expecting Him to fulfill His promises to us, is just a bit presumptuous, don't you think? If we are to understand that what Jesus said in this regard is true, any effort on our part to avail ourselves of these promises would be utter folly, and vain. Might this possibly be an explanation of why there is such a wide range of opinions and theories and interpretations of the Scriptures? Too many would-be scholars and authorities may well be far from any genuine willingness to do the will of the Father, consequently preventing them from obtaining the ability to "*know of the doctrine.*"

Jesus also said, "*Ye shall **know** the Truth...,*" not guess at it, or speculate about it, or theorize around it, "*and the truth shall make you free!*" (John 8:32) It is not necessary at all that one learn the original languages, or become proficient in the knowledge of systematic theology (although that is all very good), or be skilled in the science of hermeneutics in order to access the necessary insights and understanding to get the Word of Truth straight and hold to sound doctrine. One only needs to follow the prescribed principles which God so graciously provided for us, and He will certainly not fail to fulfill His promise. He will assuredly lead **you** into all Truth just as readily as anyone else. He will not fail to teach **you** all

Rom 12:1,2
transformed
by Renewing
mind

52

things and preserve **you** from error and deception and lies. He is utterly dependable and will not allow any of His children to flounder in a morass of deception or confusion when they come to Him in humility and trust. Can you believe Him for this?

Please bear with me because there is yet one more principle which would be most helpful to look at in conjunction with our previous discussion, which will prove most helpful in arriving at a proper understanding.

THE ORACLE

God has provided for His people virtually from day one, and for many generations preceding the generation of Christ's coming, His own very "Manifest Presence" under the provisions of the Old Covenant, the Law. That Manifest Presence first appeared, and started out with Israel as they departed from Egypt, and the Pillar of cloud by day and Fire by night accompanied and guided them unerringly for a full forty years without interruption. At the beginning of their wanderings He also provided them with a High Priest who was to wear special vestments which included something of tremendous interest. There was a breastplate of pure, worked gold included in those vestments which became for them the "Oracle" by which God made His will known to them, and answered their inquiries. There was the oracle, the Urim and Thummim, which God caused to respond in some manner when the priest made inquiry of Him. By the time Jesus was born, the Oracle had ceased to work, according to Flavius Josephus. The last of the High Priests who was able to get a response from God through the Oracle was John Hyrcanus, who was High Priest during the time of the Maccabees, the time between the Old and New Testaments. He died approximately 105 years before Jesus Christ came, and after His death no succeeding High Priest was able to get a response.

It seems that very little is known or understood concerning this Oracle, or the Urim and Thummim. There isn't much in the Bible at all concerning how it worked or what it actually did. There are a few references to it in the Old Testament for any who might wish to pursue the matter, but in no place is there any clue given as to how it worked. For such things as this we have to rely on Jewish historical records, to which we will refer shortly.

Among the rest of His instructions to Moses, God gave a description and pattern for the High Priest's vestments. This office of High Priest was clearly a type of the coming Messiah (Exodus 29). The breastplate was a significant, major part of these vestments, and was made of pure, 24kt worked gold, with twelve large gemstones inlaid in it, each one representing one of the twelve tribes of Israel. They were arranged in three rows of four each. Then there were two large Onyx stones on the shoulders, to which the gold chains of the breast plate were attached. Each of these stones had the names of six of the tribes engraved on it. Something pertaining to this breastplate was called by God "the Urim and Thummim", which by translation means "lights and perfections". Some think that the Urim and Thummim was something either added to the breastplate, or possibly included with it in some manner, maybe in a pouch of some kind. Some suggest that these may have been two additional gemstones of some kind which were not identified. This whole setup is what became known as the "Oracle". It has been established and taught by Bible scholars over the centuries, from the very earliest history of the Church that this Urim and Thummim, or Lights and Perfections, were a clear picture of the New Testament testimony of the Word and the Spirit combined. These two, the Word and the Spirit, are in fact our "Oracle" today, and are most definitely available to any and all true believers who will pursue to avail themselves of their function. It is by means of these that we, the true and genuine sons of God, the "Royal Priesthood", are made to know and understand His judgments and His will.

According to Flavius Josephus, an ancient Jewish historian from the time of the Apostle Paul, as well as others, this Oracle was so named by the Greeks (probably Alexander the Great, himself) who were quite impressed by its awesome function. He states that this Oracle responded supernaturally when the High Priest stood before the Lord at the veil in front of the Holy of Holies, and inquired of Him. He says that the response came by means of the onyx stones ("sardonyx" in some translations), upon the shoulders of the priest, when they would light up with a brilliant and "surprising" radiance. On some notable occasions recorded by Josephus, its brightness was so intense, described by him as "…bright rays darting out thence!", that it could be seen at the farthest reaches of the camp of the Israelites. He also noted that all twelve stones in the breastplate shone with so great a splendor that all of the people were sensible of Gods being present with them for their assistance.

There also seemed to be, as he implied, a clear correlation between the spiritual status of the High Priest, his acceptableness before God, and the intensity of the response. Josephus noted that it left off shining because God was displeased at the transgression of His Law. This John Hyrcanus was considered by Josephus to have been both prophet and king, as well as High Priest! It was most interestingly noted also, that when the Lord was inquired of by this means, and the stones shone with such brilliance at His response, there was an accompanying audible voice which spoke supernaturally from the Mercy Seat, which was the lid of the Ark of the Covenant, from between the Cherubim, from behind the veil. (All of this information can be found in the Works of Josephus, Book III, Ch. 8 ¶ 9, for any who wish to examine this more thoroughly).

From the time of the death of John Hyrcanus to this very day the Jews have had no means of confirming the judgments and will of God by the working of the Urim and Thummim, but now only by mere human interpretation of the written Word which they accept. That is, unless

59

they should turn to Jesus and receive the Holy Spirit's fullness, and learn to avail themselves of that of which the original Urim and Thummim was a type! It was, to a great extent, because of the failing of the Oracle before Jesus' day due to their many transgressions and their backslidden state that the Jews were unable to verify and validate, or identify their Messiah when He presented Himself to them. The mere human, intellectual, academic approach to understanding the prophecies proved to be devastatingly inadequate and insufficient! Their transgressions of God's Law, not willing to do the will of the Father, had rendered them unable to make that Oracle work for them, so that it not only rendered them unable to recognize their Messiah, but also caused them to tragically become the very ones responsible for killing Him!

The same principle applies to God's people, the church, today! The bulk of Christianity which calls itself Fundamental, Evangelcal, Conservative, Orthodox, etc., has sadly succumbed to

60

the prevailing spirit of the age, and has become a
religion based primarily on Theological "Theories" *~what*
and doctrinal positions, presenting debates and
contests between all the various positions! Most
seem to have lost any of the "Manifest Presence
of God", which not only produces souls with a
spiritual quality which has been described as *"on
fire"*, but which also produces access to the New
Testament fulfillment of the Oracle! It appears
that too many of us have forgotten the words
of the Apostle Paul, under the direct inspira- *Be*
tion of the Holy Spirit, in I Cor. 4:20, that "...*the* *careful*
Kingdom of God is not in word but in POWER*"!!
So little valid "discerning of spirits" is practiced
anywhere, which helps account for the incredible profusion of doctrines, and of false teachers
and preachers and false 'ministers of righteousness', all making their incursion into the church.
It can account for the fact that so many problem
men end up in the pulpits of our churches today,
leading so many astray.

61

Left only with mere human intellect and the degenerate condition of the carnal mind of Adam's nature to discern and interpret the prophecies of Scripture, those Jews tragically missed their promised Savior and Redeemer! They became the very fulfillment of the prophecies they thought they knew but could not really understand because of their transgressions! Because of their willful blindness and ignorance, John found it necessary to say of them, *"He was in the world, and the world was made by Him, and the world knew Him not. He came unto His own, and His own received Him not"* (John 1:10 & 11). They unceremoniously brushed Him aside and shoved Him out of their way so they could continue looking diligently and carefully, with their intellect and academics intact, for someone they could accept as their promised Messiah, without any of these troublesome distractions! But much to their dismay, the 483rd year of Daniel's prophecy came and went, and they missed Him completely and utterly! Today, many of the Jews do not even unroll the scroll of Daniel to read it because it disturbs them so much. One Rabbi said, "Too many predictions!"

There is a very serious lesson to be learned from this! The "Manifest Presence" of God seems to be at least as hard to find in much of His church today as it was then! There are great numbers of knowledgeable, intellectual, academically prepared scholars studying and looking to the events of prophecy for our day, many of them fully convinced, and no doubt properly so, that this is, indeed, the very time, the very generation of His return. But might there not be very few who are of the nature of a Simeon, of an Anna, who will actually have the "instant recognition" of the events as they occur? How many will actually **know** their Christ when He appears again? It appears that the spiritual state today is very much like that of the time of Christ's earthly ministry! Prophecy actually says it will be that way.

63

Much of the contents of all the popular books on this subject are in the category of "interpretive theory", or "speculative opinion", and they are not to be accepted as inspired, holy writ. That is not at all difficult to see, because there are so many widely varied opinions and conclusions. They cannot, therefore, be said to be given by revelation of the Holy Spirit - the *Oracle* - the Manifest Presence of God! There are at least five interpretive theories or speculative opinions concerning the identity of the Two Witnesses of Revelation 11. There have been, and yet are, all kinds of ideas and speculations concerning the identity of the "Antichrist" - the Beast - and the false prophet, and the circumstances surrounding their appearance. There is much speculation and supposition surrounding the identification of the ten toes of Nebuchadnezzar's dream and the ten horns of the Beast of Revelation, and the various proposed speculative identifications are, at best, highly questionable! The popular theories of the identity of the "Babylon" of Revelation are only that, "theories", and are not, as all the rest, to be construed as Truth inspired of God, as some would seem to be trying to have us believe. Any new or contrary approach which casts doubt on these popular theories is not necessarily to be regarded as heresy or error.

Be careful

Many of the facts of prophecy are, indeed, recognizable by even the most cursory reading of the Scriptures, but many of these facts could well be so misinterpreted or misunderstood by so many scholars due to the absence of the Oracle, so that when the prophecies are fulfilled an awful lot of people will fail to recognize them as a legitimate part of prophetic fulfillment! Many will doubtless be just as fooled and surprised by the people and events which are a part of actual fulfillment as those were in Christ's day, but with potentially far more devastating and terrifying results! The Word of God is still true, and is yet fulfilled in this regard when it says, "*...the ignorant and unstable twist and misconstrue to*

Be careful of anything contrary to the clear meaning of the Written Word.

yes

their destruction, just as they distort and misrepresent the rest of the Scriptures!" (II Peter 3:16 Amplified). Those who have become so enamored by theorizing or the theoretical approach to Biblical interpretation will **never** get it straight, simply because they can't.

Beware

What about the doctrine of the "rapture" of the church? There are numerous theories and opinions and interpretations concerning this important prophetic event. If the translation of the saints should happen to occur in any manner or at any time other than every believer departing this world supernaturally immediately preceding the seven year "great tribulation", it will prove to be a horribly devastating experience for a great majority of Christians today! They could well all wake up some day and find themselves right in the midst of the greatest time of tribulation and testing of faith the world has ever experienced! The prospect of encountering something of that nature without any expectation, and

66

consequently no preparation, would likely prove extremely devastating and tragic!

The five most common theories concerning this "rapture" of the church leave the honest inquisitive student more than a bit confused. The word "rapture" does not even occur in the Scripture, even in relation to this event, making it impossible to pursue or trace this doctrine by that means through a concordance. The word "rapture", itself, means literally "the ultimate heights of ecstasy or joy", which may very well describe the effects of this event on the true saints. But the event is never referred to by that terminology in the Scripture. However, the event is reported specifically in I Thessalonians 4:13-18, and is alluded to in some other passages.

There are some scholars who question, with some seemingly adequate Scriptural support, whether such an event will even occur. They call into question the common interpretation of the Scriptures which are applied by others to a catching away of the saints.

67

The majority opinion or theory of conservative and evangelical theologians is that this translation will occur as the event which ushers in the final seven years of this dispensation, which is called "the Great Tribulation". There are others, and their numbers seem to be growing, who suggest that it will occur at the midpoint of the tribulation period, three and a half years into it. Yet another group is quite convinced that it is scheduled to occur at the conclusion of the seven years. I have even heard some say that they thought there might well be a series of "raptures" or translations occurring throughout that seven year period.

There are other variations on these themes, no doubt, but it should be obvious that there can only be one actual Truth concerning the matter! Nothing whatsoever is to be gained by all of this theorizing with its interpretive contortions! Only the "lights and Perfections", the "Oracle" of the New Testament system, can make this Truth known for certain! Any other attempt, through any other process, is quite obviously inadequate for obtaining the actual knowledge on this matter, just as with any other matter! Each differing opinion is held and propagated by men and women who are recognized for their high credentials and standards of achievement in their intellectual, academic, and theoretical accomplishments. And yet no more than one position can possibly be right! With all of their great academic achievements and diligent study, they are all as yet unable to come to an agreement with each other, and are unable to bring to fulfillment the admonition of I Cor.1:10. Paul noted that *"spiritual things are spiritually discerned," (*I Cor. 2:14) so if we approach the obtaining of spiritual truths by the use of carnal or fleshly means, we are doomed to failure! Spiritual things are **only** spiritually discerned. Whenever there is a wide discrepancy in any matter of biblical understanding or interpretation, appeal must be made to the Oracle for a response, or for a testimony to the Truth. It is the Spirit of Truth alone Who can lead us into *all truth,* just as Jesus promised. It was by this principle **alone** that Simeon and Anna were enabled to recognize that little eight day old infant as their promised Messiah, while the proud intellectuals of the theological world utterly failed to recognize Him and ultimately rejected and killed Him, in spite of all the signs and evidences He displayed right before their very eyes!

So it remains that if the actual Truth concerning the rapture is anything other than the popular 'pre-tribulation rapture' *theory*, there will be many millions who will be horribly shocked and totally unprepared for what they are about to face, and thoroughly dismayed as they end up going through the most arduous test of their faith imaginable.

(I would like to insert here a brief parenthetical observation. The apostle Paul tells us, under the inspiration of the Holy Ghost, that this event will occur in conjunction with the "first resurrection" (I Thess. 4:15-17), and at the time of the sounding of "...*the last trump*..." (I Corinthians 15:52). There is only one "...*last* trump"! There can only <u>be</u> one "...*last* trump"! If there should be any other trumpet sounding later, then this one could not be called the "last"! This **last** trump, then it seems, would have to be the one which we are told sounds right after the account of the "Two Witnesses" finishing their testimony, at the end of the first three and a half years of the tribulation period, recorded in Revelation 11. There is no other reference whatsoever to any other sounding of any other trumpet or trumpets in relation to the time of the end, in any other corroborating passage. The only trumpets mentioned in the book of Revelation are the seven which the seven angels sound near the end of the first half of the tribulation, with the seventh, or **last** one, sounding just as these "two witnesses" are called to "... come up hither...!")

There is still one more prospect we need to examine in relation to these matters. As previously noted, the Messiah was expected to appear at that time in a particular manner and fashion which had been calculated and determined by all Bible scholars and contemporary students of prophecy of the day. However, when He actually *did* appear, it was in a manner just enough different than they had figured out that they *couldn't* recognize Him!

In our day we are watching for the prophesied "Antichrist", who is expected by our contemporary scholars and students of prophecy to appear in a particular manner or fashion, and from a particular place or locale. What might be the possibility that the majority of our scholars today are approaching their understanding and interpretation of the Scriptures pertaining to this one in the same general manner, using similar methods of interpretation as those scholars in Christ's day, without access to the Urim and Thummim, and are missing some vital pieces of understanding which would be needed to give them the ability to recognize him when he actually arrives on the scene?

Would it not, then, be quite likely that they would be thrown off the track and fail to recognize him, very much in the same way as those in Christ's day? What, then, could be the potential prospects? Might not it then be possible, or even likely, that these very students of prophecy and their adherents could become admirers or even followers of this very one they have been warning about for years? If they have missed something of importance because of the failure or inability or neglect to access the New Testament Oracle, might not their understanding be sufficiently diluted to bring this about? The common expectations are that he will either rise to power in the Middle East, or in the current European Community. A man like Saddam Hussein had become a prime suspect for those who expect this one to come out of the Middle East. So much for that theory. The Pope in Rome is a very prominent prospect for those who are looking for him to rise up from within the European Community. Others would identify the Pope as the "False

Prophet" rather than the "Antichrist". (We will discuss this more fully a little further on.) Quite a few names have been bantered around for quite a number of years, and many are even projected yet today of a "type" of person expected to become this "antichrist".

Such expectations are all based on interpretive theories, or on mere speculation, but a very large segment of the church is banking on it being that way. After all, the authorities are all saying it will occur like this. What would be the results, however, if he should instead come to power, say, right here in the USA as a marvelous moral, religious political leader who produces and accomplishes peace like no other has ever done before? He could ease into his place as the "antichrist" completely unsuspected, even possibly touted by many good Evangelical Christians, because he didn't come from the right part of the world. After all, "*No prophet ever arises out of Galilee!*"

74

These suggestions are not mere speculations or foolish ponderings or theories! Such kinds of things have happened before, as when Christ arrived under such clear prophetic statements as then, what reason do we have to not expect that it could happen again in our time?! The Lord *did* tell us that even the *"very elect"* would be deceived, if it were possible for them to be deceived! *"For false Christs and false prophets will arise, and they will show great signs and wonders so as to deceive and lead astray, if possible, even the elect (God's chosen ones)."* (Matt. 24:24 AMP)

That would seem to imply, would it not, that this character would be a rather marvelous replica of morality and godliness. I know of no true believer who would ever come close to being fooled by anyone like a Saddam, or the Pope, or a Khadafy, or anyone else of their ilk! The genuine "very elect" are really too smart to fall for any of these kinds of people. If they are to be even potentially deceived, it would virtually

75

have to be by someone who was more closely likened to Christ. The potential prospects of this kind of deception are truly frightening!

With this background of thinking, and with these thoughts in mind, there are several different directions we could turn. But one passage which seems to have been mostly overlooked by students and scholars may hold a very important key to this whole picture. The prophecies of Daniel are most fascinating, and picture some most intriguing possibilities. Not all of his prophecies are even alluded to by many of the current scholars as relating to end times. But a closer examination may reveal some most fascinating, even possibly startling things.

Daniel was instructed by the angel who spoke with him to at the very end of the book *"...shut up the words and seal the book <u>until the time of the end...</u>"* (Dan. 12:4). Then he was told a short time later, "*...the words <u>are</u> shut up and sealed <u>until the time of the end</u>*". It is quite obvious that the book has not been hidden or secreted away some place. It has been available for reading from its origin, and has been included in the canon of Scripture for many, many centuries, so these statements were not to be understood to mean that it was to be hidden from view for all these years. The prophecies of Daniel were "sealed" by the Spirit of God, preventing anyone from understanding their full implications "*...until the time of the end*". They were not intended by God to be understood until this very period of time in which we are now living! Understanding and knowledge pertaining to their end time significance was intended by God to be withheld from any and all searchers until God, Himself, by the Holy Spirit, "The Oracle", would open that seal, and *"open our understandings that we might understand the Scriptures"* (Luke 24:45). Any attempt or effort prior to God's chosen time to examine into these matters would prove vain and unfruitful. No amount of academic or hermeneutical efforts could ever break that seal before God was ready for it to be broken. Then,

77

it would <u>not</u> be by those means that it would be broken, but by means of the "oracle", the "Lights and Perfections"! Even now, any attempt to understand these things apart from the Oracle would be futile.

NEBUCHADNEZZAR'S DREAM

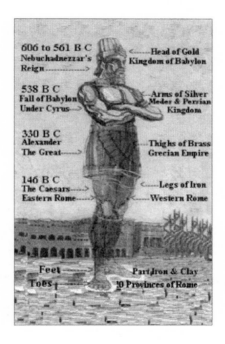

With all this in mind, it is time to take a look at the very first prophecy of this book. This prophecy was quite unique in that it was actually given by way of a dream to the Babylonian king, Nebuchadnezzar, who could not even remember it, let alone interpret or understand it (Daniel 2). But Daniel, just a youth probably still in his teens, was given by God the full knowledge of the dream, as well as its interpretation! Take note that none of this information was even possible to obtain by any academic, scholarly, or intellectual pursuits.

This dream and its interpretation are well known to Bible students. The dream was of a great image of a man, composed of five elements. The head was of gold; the shoulders and arms were silver; the belly and thighs were brass; the legs were iron; and the feet and toes were a mix of iron mingled with clay. In the dream, a stone was hewn out without human hands, and rolled down to the image, smiting it in its feet, and then continuing to roll over the rest of the image, pulverizing all the rest of the elements *all at the same time*. That stone then grew to be a huge mountain which filled the entire earth.

The interpretation given by God to Daniel, again apart from any academic or intellectual pursuits, speaks of the various parts of the image as representative of five great kingdoms which were to rule successively over the whole world. They were each to be world dominating, world-ruling kingdoms. These have all been rather easily and satisfactorily identified as 1) Babylon, 2) Medo-Persia, 3) Greece, 4) Rome, and 5) a final, unidentified kingdom. The stone, then, is identified as a kingdom which God, Himself, will set up over the whole earth after utterly destroying all remnants of the previous kingdoms. This kingdom is said to then be "*...given to the people of the saints of the Most High God...*" (Daniel 7:27), and is clearly referring to the Millennial Kingdom of Christ at the end of time. No great mystery here it seems. Babylon rose to great power, and then was conquered by Medo-Persia; Medo-Persia came and went; Greece conquered, and then were themselves conquered; Rome supplanted Greece, and then fell from within without being defeated. The final kingdom has not yet been revealed, or yet (maybe?) come to power.

81

But something in this narrative has seemingly been overlooked! Something of rather major importance and significance seems to have been missed! The Stone which smote the image in its feet (an event apparently yet to come) proceeded immediately, *at the very same time*, to crush and grind to dust "...*the iron, the clay, the bronze, the silver, and the gold, broken and crushed together!*" (Daniel 2:35). Then, in the interpretation, in v. 44, Daniel declares (all quotes from the Amplified Bible), that the kingdom which God sets up shall "...*crush and consume all these kingdoms*..." It is quite obvious that "...*all these kingdoms*,,," must yet exist in the world today in some fashion or form, and until that day when the stone smites the image in its feet, and the God of Heaven sets up His kingdom on the Earth! This means that Babylon yet exists somewhere, in some form, as do Medo-Persia, Greece, and Rome! Who are they now? Where are they? What are they?!

82

There are some clues in the book of Revelation. This book is predominantly a prophecy relating to and covering the final seven years of this age, and leads into a brief prophetic picture of the Millennium. "Babylon" is spoken of in chapter 18 as falling, or being destroyed, much to the horror of the whole world, during the time of this great tribulation period. The description of the fall of this "Babylon" is a very graphic picture of a monetary or economic collapse which *Religious* is worldwide in scope. Merchants are suddenly, "*in a day*", wiped out! There is nobody left who can buy their goods! Merchant ships at sea carrying goods to ports at various locations around the world are suddenly stranded, and there is no place they can dock to unload their cargo of goods! There is a very lengthy description of the kinds of results which occur all around the world when this Babylon falls.

There has been much conjecture and speculation as to the identity of the "Babylon" of Revelation. The predominant opinion seems to have been that it relates to the Roman Catholic Church. It is assumed by many that, among other factors, because this Babylon is described as sitting on seven hills, and Rome has been said to have been built on seven hills, that this clearly equates the two. (San Francisco is also said to be built on seven hills, by the way.) Many efforts have been made by many Bible scholars to support this equation, but there is a major problem to be encountered here. If the whole Catholic Church were to be destroyed in one fell swoop, would world economy react in the manner depicted in Revelation 18?! I don't think so! I doubt it would even cause much more than a ripple, an economic stutter.

Recently some have jumped on the bandwagon of trying to identify Saddam Hussein's attempted rebuilding of ancient Babylon with this Babylon of Revelation 18. Iraq doesn't even have within it the seeds of potential destruction of the entire world economy in the manner described in Revelation 18. They made a feeble effort during the Gulf War to wrack up the world, dumping huge quantities of oil into the sea, setting lots of oil wells on fire, ravaging a land, etc., but it hardly made a stutter. If Iraq and Saddam were to be totally annihilated tomorrow, I doubt seriously that the kind of things described in Revelation 18 would *ever* occur, and the world economy would very likely continue mostly unabated.

No, the Babylon of Revelation must be identified with something which, if destroyed or suffering collapse, would bring about the effects described here. And I would suggest that it must be tied into and related in some way with the ancient Babylonian Head of gold.

The Babylon of Daniel was characterized in the dream by the element of gold. Ancient Babylon under Nebuchadnezzar was fabulously wealthy! It built the most famous "hanging gardens", which became one of the seven wonders of the ancient world! It made obvious the tremendous wealth of that kingdom! The great image which the king set up (chap. 3) which was

85

90 feet high and 9 feet wide was made of _solid gold,_ another pretty good indicator.

But that gold stood for something more than just wealth. It is a fact of history that Babylon, under that famous king, established a new system of commerce and trade. They originated a monetary and economic system hitherto unknown to the world. Goods and services could be obtained by means of money in a system which started the whole economic and monetary principle under which the world is now operating. Prior to this time, even though coins were struck and used to some extent, commerce was conducted primarily by barter or trade. This new system became the standard for the world for all ages to come, including the age in which we now find ourselves. We are now, in other words, living under the very system of Babylon! This system may have been somewhat modified from time to time depending on existing circumstances and situations, but it has remained essentially the same as when it was originated under the head of gold!

Is it not true, then, that the Babylon of today, in its end-time connotation, is this very economic, monetary system which was left to us as a legacy by the original Babylon? It is quite certain that if or when *this* Babylonian economic and monetary system should collapse, the results would be just as depicted in Revelation 18. Is there really any other possible identity which could even come close to producing those results?

This system as it is today has an identity - a location from which it operates and is controlled. The current monetary system of the world has a central place of administration and control. The seat of control for the World Bank, for the World Trade Center, and the center of operations for World Commerce, is located in New York City! The man who serves as president of the World Bank is appointed to that position by the President of the United States. The World Trade center Buildings, one of which was damaged by a bomb several years ago, and then both were destroyed on 9/11/2001 is in New

87

York City. The World Monetary system is controlled by Wall Street, in New York City. The American dollar is the world's standard in all of the monetary markets of the world. As goes the American dollar and Stock Market, so goes the currency and stock markets of the rest of the world. There can be little doubt but that the Economic and Monetary system of the world is literally under the control of the USA. It is rather obvious, I would think, that the Babylon of the End Times is based and centered right here in this country, not geographically in the same place as it was originally.

What, then, about Medo-Persia? Unlike Babylon, Medo-Persia is not mentioned by name in Revelation, and no reference is made to its fall or destruction. But we found the identity of Babylon by finding and tracing what of Babylon was transmitted down through the centuries virtually intact to the present day! We were able to trace the origin of the economic and monetary system back through time to its beginnings in ancient Babylon. Might we not be able to identify the other parts of the image in a similar manner, by applying the same principle or using the same approach?

Medo-Persia was an interesting kingdom. It was inferior in some respects to the Babylonian kingdom it replaced, as silver is inferior to gold. But what did they contribute to all of posterity that is still in operation today? Did they originate anything which became a part of succeeding civilizations? They took control of the existing monetary system, and the trade and commerce of the world, and they produced their own coinage, but the system, itself, was Babylonian in all respects. Did they, however, contribute anything new?

Throughout all of history from the time of that second kingdom, a proverb has passed from generation to generation, *"the law of the Medes and Persians"*. I recall my own Father, when he was making a point that he had issued his final decree on a matter concerning my required obedience, would utter that little phrase, "... it's the law of the Medes and Persians". They established a system of <u>government by law</u>, not merely by king's decree. I am sure they may well have borrowed some of their ideas from other sources, but it remained for them to establish the system which bears their name and stamp - *"The Law of the Medes and Persians"*! In this system, once a law was decreed and signed into effect, it could not be altered or set aside or abridged, even by the king himself! The people had recourse <u>only</u> to the law, <u>not</u> to the king, nor to any other man or committee of men! Daniel, himself, found out about this in a later experience. The law was decreed that nobody in the kingdom could bow down or offer prayers to any god or man other than the ruling king, Darius the Mede, for thirty days. The punishment for any violation was decreed that the offender was to be cast into a den of lions. The passage concerning this, in Daniel 6, makes mention of "the law of the Medes and Persians" which cannot be altered even by the king himself. It states that the king tried all day to find some loophole, a way to deliver Daniel, and could not! The law had been decreed and signed, and could not be set aside even by the king! Daniel's deliverance was left only to the hand of God.

Esther also experienced the effects of this system under Ahasuerus, or Xerxes, the Persian king (see Esther 3:8 through 8:14). He was conned into signing a decree for the destruction of the Jews and could do nothing about the decree once it had been set in motion. The only thing he could do was to make and sign another decree giving the Jews the right to take up arms to defend themselves, making any attempt to kill them too costly to try. The Law of the Medes and Persians was clearly depicted in these episodes.

Might we not possibly identify the Medo-Persia of the end times by determining where this system of "government by law" is rooted and centered today?! Is there a place on this earth where the system introduced by the Medes and Persians is in effect today, recognizable, and where people appeal to law in all matters of social importance? Of course there is! And the entire world is aware of it. No other people or nation today is as noted for this system as are we, right here, again, in the United States of America. This nation was established on the very principle of which we are speaking. We are very accustomed to this form of justice. Although true justice has its serious problems today in our society, its principle is yet with us here, as in no other place, and any man in any station of life has the privilege of appeal to the law. Even in this day, in a world which is supposedly in an advanced stage of civilization, this is rare. The Medo-Persia of the "time of the end" is certain to be identified with the United States of America!

The original kingdom of the Medes and Persians was eventually conquered by Alexander the Great of Greece, and the third element of the image of Nebuchadnezzar's dream came to power. The Greeks continued

92

with the Babylonian system of coinage and commerce, and functioned pretty much according to the Medo-Persian system of law. But this people added something else to subsequent history which can be found and identified in this present time - "the time of the end".

Their contribution was actually twofold, the belly and the two thighs. First, they were a nation of philosophers, ardent seekers after wisdom and knowledge. Some of their people traveled throughout the entire known world seeking for expanded knowledge to the greatest extent possible for them. One man, Solon by name, traveled to Egypt and spent several years obtaining all the ancient wisdom of the Egyptians that he could gain from their priests and scholars. He returned to Greece several years later and passed this information and knowledge on to other philosophers and scholars of Greece.

In their worship of intellect and their unending quest for "truth" and the love of reason (philosophy), they originated something which caught

93

on, and which has continued in the civilizations and societies of the world right through all the ages of time, on down to the very present, this "time of the end". Up until their time, education was primarily the responsibility of each family, individually. Fathers taught their sons the learning of the day, or else sent them to the patriarch of the family to learn from him. In Greece, these great philosophic minds began to accumulate and gather around themselves young men from their society whom they taught from their own resources and expertise. This gave birth to a new approach to education, producing an educational system with which we have become familiar! Like no people before them, they popularized this quest for knowledge and wisdom, and made it available to the general populace, and propagated it in a manner which can be traced through all of subsequent history. Literally every civilization adopted this approach.

But that is not the only contribution the Greeks made to civilization. Their very brilliant philosophers reasoned that war was the product of man's need to conquer, or compete, or to show himself equal or superior to anyone else. If something could be substituted for warfare and killing, maybe then war and killing could be eradicated. So they instituted and launched the famous Olympic Games, named for Mount Olympus, the home of all their gods. Athletic competition became an integral part of society and civilization from that time on. It was certainly more civil to attempt to outdo someone else in running, either for speed or endurance, and jumping, and throwing, and wrestling, and boxing, etc., than it was to kill! The competitive events of the very first Olympic Games are still with us and in effect today, along with a plethora of other competitive activities.

Now, where else in the world will we find this combination of education and athletic competition as prominently as, once again, right here in the USA! Both are major parts of our society and civilization. There is no other nation or people on the face of the earth which has promoted free thinking in education, and has encouraged all kinds of philosophies, and has even taught that way in the educational system, and at the same time is so athletically active from the earliest years of a child's development as we are right here in the good ol' USA! Regimented totalitarian societies such as those who have been under Communist domination, may promote education, but have been extremely intolerant and restrictive of any deviation from the official established philosophy of the party in power, very unlike the Greeks. Our national policy of freedom of thought and expression, though suffering quite a bit currently, much more closely imitates that of the ancient Greeks than that of any other culture currently in existence. By far the predominant numbers of nations of the world send their youth to this country to educate them. The vast majority of emerging third world countries have leaders who were educated right here in this country.

96

What about the Greek approach to athletic competition? In the last several years of international competition, athletes from our country have been challenged by athletes from some of these regimented, totalitarian societies which seem to be producing more outstanding athletes. But the process of producing these "super athletes" must be considered. They are, for the most part, automatons, mere robots of the state, and have had little or no real choice in what they do or how they do it. They are drafted without opportunity for appeal, after being run through tests to determine their natural abilities, and then they are put into a program of regimented training, shown to have often also included performance enhancing drugs. This, then, becomes their life, their employment, their profession, their service to their country for as long as they are able to maintain the necessary performance level. There has never been, and is not now, a nation which produces the quantity and overall quality of athletes at every level of competition as this great nation of ours, and all voluntarily. The large number of people involved in athletic competition at every age level in our society, from pre-school, through school and in all kinds of amateur and professional sports is unprecedented in the history of the world! If any part of the images fits contemporary USA, the Bronze of Greece most certainly does.

Next we come to the legs of iron - Rome. The influence of the previous three can be plainly seen here. The Romans really got into the "games", and built huge coliseums to engage in them, and expanded them into great public events. They really took them to extremes.

But now another factor enters into the picture. Rome is depicted in the dream as being represented by the element of iron, and as it is stated that even as iron breaks in pieces everything else, even so shall this kingdom break and crush all others around it (Daniel 2:40). Rome became noted for its mighty military power. They certainly didn't originate warfare or fighting, and may not have even been the best fighting force in the world. But they did something with military combat which had never been done before. They devised and established a system of warfare involving troops, legions, battalions, etc. - a "chain of command". This system and its accompanying tactics of warfare were unique, and were so effective that even to this day that system is taught in our own military academies, and is studied and used by our military tacticians. (I was told this directly by a man who was a two-star General of the U. S. Air Force.) Modern warfare still uses the very system invented by the Romans! Rome conquered and maintained their conquests by means of their superior military tactics and strategies rather than by their superiority of fighting forces, and they were never defeated! Their "defeat" was from internal corruption, not from external conquest. They were not toppled from without, but fell from within!

There has been much discussion over the past several years concerning who is the greatest military power in the world today. Is it China with their vast superiority in numbers? Is it possibly Russia and all of her erstwhile allies? Or is it the United States of America? Many pages have been written, and are still being written, to support the contention that the Russians and Chinese have equaled us, or even surpassed us, in their military capabilities. Their "might", however, is subject to serious questions, especially now in the wake of the recent events in the dismantling of the former Soviet Union.

It is a rather well established and well known fact that the Russians have been, for many years, masters in the art of bluffing. Even in their own Communist literature, which has been in print for most of this century, they declare that they have never intended to conquer the world through military might. It is quite well known that they have boasted that they would take this country without ever having to fire a shot! Their intention was to undermine our will and moral character through many different means, until we would just fall into their hands like an overripe fruit! All they needed to do was to simply maintain just enough of a military front or appearance to convince us that they could retaliate sufficiently to deter us. They acted like bullies, and bluffed their way through their downfall.

Oh, they unquestionably possess enough to wreak a lot of havoc in the world, but when comparing them with the USA, they fall far short! Every single time they were confronted by us in any situation, and were told they had gone too far, and we held our ground in demanding that they stop or back down, they always acceded to our demands, albeit with much rhetoric and blustering and complaining. They became master propagandists, and succeeded in persuading the rest of the world that they were far more capable than they really were. This worked to their great advantage in all kinds of negotiations with other nations, including ours. They managed to obtain many concessions by this means, maintaining this propaganda stature. When you think about it, it also worked to the advantage of our own Pentagon and military hierarchy to go along with this propaganda. They could capitalize on it in obtaining greater consideration for appropriations for further development and acquisition of improved military hardware.

This very brief and simple declaration is no proof of anything. It would require at the least an entire chapter just to present the minimal facts and information which are in my own possession to support these contentions. And it would require an entire book to present all the evidence which is available, and several volumes if we were to be able to include classified information which is not readily available. But the evidence does exist, and it would satisfactorily prove that we are, indeed, the greatest military power in the world today and in fact the greatest in the entire history of the world. It is a fact that the technology of the Russian military and all its allies is considerably behind ours, and their production of quality military hardware cannot compare to what we have. It is my opinion, as well as the opinion of others who are much more in the know, that they would require, under near ideal conditions, anywhere from ten to twelve years minimum to even approach the level where we are right now. A leading member of our Senate Armed Services Committee recently spoke on the radio to his constituents and made some very similar observations, to the effect that if we were to totally stop our production and research, it would likely take as much as *twenty* years for them to just catch up with us.

I do believe, however, that it would be a grave mistake to allow ourselves to ever become complacent, resulting in reduced vigilance. It is certainly to our advantage that we continue to act as though we felt we were on shaky ground. But in examining the prophecies with which we are dealing, there is every positive reason to equate this nation with the latter day legs of iron of the image of Nebuchadnezzar's dream! There is, in fact, other evidence in Scripture to support this proposition that in the time of the end *one* nation is representative of the *whole* image! We will take a look at that shortly.

Before relegating these propositions to the scrap heap of far-out or strange speculations being presented by some sensationalist, there is considerably more Scriptural evidence which must be taken into account in *any* interpretation - evidence which seems to have been overlooked or ignored, or just simply missed thus far by virtually *all* writers on the subject of end-time prophecy. We shall not proceed to the feet and toes of the image - the final kingdom - until we have looked at this other evidence as thoroughly as the evidence warrants.

DANIEL'S VISION

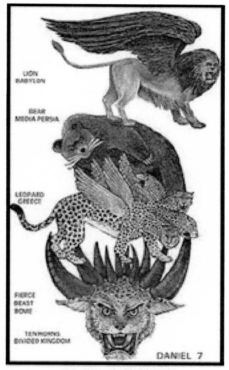

The Beasts of Daniel 7

This dream and its interpretation were further corroborated to Daniel somewhat later in his life, during the first year of

Belshazzar, the last of the kings of Babylon. The Lord this time gave Daniel "*A dream and visions...*" (Ch. 7:1), in which he was shown four beasts or creatures similar to animals, but peculiar in many respects. These four beasts are very clearly identified to Daniel as correlating with the various elements of the image of Nebuchadnezzar's dream. There was a lion which represented Babylon. Then there was a bear which represented Med-Persia. Then a leopard is shown, which represented Greece. Finally there was the indescribably terrible beast which represented Rome, as well as the unnamed future, final kingdom, or "kingdoms". All of these beasts were supplanted by "the Son of Man" who was given "...*dominion, glory, and kingdom...*" (vs. 13, 14). Note, also, verses 26 and 27, which declare that, the "...*sovereignty, the dominion, and the greatness of **all** the kingdoms under the whole Heaven [the entire world] will be given to '... **the people** of the saints of the Highest One...*'", etc. All of these kingdoms, represented by the beasts *and* the image of Nebuchadnezzar's dream, will be destroyed <u>*all together, at one point of time*</u>, and will be given to <u>*the people of God*</u>! The Millennial kingdom, the stone which crushed the other kingdoms then filled the whole earth, will be ruled by Christ **and** His saints! The ten toes of the image and the ten horns of the indescribably terrible beast are references to the final world kingdom(s) and the "antichrist" which arises out of them. When this reigning kingdom is destroyed by the stone, God's people, under Christ, will be given to rule over the whole earth for a thousand years.

There is even further evidence yet in Daniel in another vision he is given of a ram and a he-goat, described in Ch. 8. These two are clearly identified to him as representing the two kingdoms of Medo-Persia and Greece, according to the understanding given to him by the angel Gabriel in vs. 20 & 21, "*The ram which thou sawest having two horns are the kings of Media and Persia. The rough goat is*

107

the king of Grecia: and the great horn which is between his eyes is the first king." He had been previously told in v. 17 that this vision was for *"...the time of the end..."*, or *"...the final period of indignation..."* (V.19). Verse 26 in this passage declares that this particular vision *"...pertains to <u>many days in the future</u>..."*, and that the vision must remain "shut up", or "sealed up" until that time. (See the Amplified version). This particular vision is all about Medo-Persia and Greece, with nothing of Rome appearing. In our days, these kingdoms of ancient significance are of no particular consequence now, and yet out of the goat, or Greece, in the "time of the end", comes one who will perform in a manner which is very descriptive of the one who comes out of the ten horns of the indescribably terrible beast, "Rome", and is quite commonly identified as "the Antichrist". Are these actually two different individuals living and operating in the same period of time - the Beast and the false prophet? Or might they not be the same individual being referred to in two different prophetic visions concerning the same event? Before drawing any final conclusions on the matter, let's look at some further Scriptural evidence.

We noted earlier that the book of Revelation, though making rather extensive mention of Babylon by name, and describing in fairly lengthy detail its fall and destruction, makes no mention of any of the other kingdoms by name. It seems rather strange that this should be the case if, as Daniel states, these kingdoms are all a part of the end which John covers rather thoroughly in the book of Revelation. Is it possible that John may have overlooked or missed something? Or might it be that God withheld something from John which has been revealed to Daniel?! This is very unlikely.

Revelation 13 describes a very strange beast which John described as coming up out of the sea. This beast is a composite of different animals with which we are already acquainted. It is

109

first described as having ten horns, like the fourth beast of Daniel's vision. It is also described as having seven heads, something of a variation from Daniel's beast, it seems. It is then described as being like a leopard (Greece), with feet like a bear (Medo-Persia), with a mouth like a lion (Babylon). All five elements are present in this *one* composite creature! All five kingdoms come together into *one* entity in the time of the end!

This is still not the end of the picture, however! In v. 11, John sees yet another beast resembling a ram with two horns, a different beast from the composite, who exercises all the authority of the first beast (v. 12). He, the ram, has the power to perform miracles and signs in deceiving the whole earth (even the "very elect", if that were possible), directing everyone to the other beast by all his efforts. This quite clearly depicts the false prophet who is to work side by side with the Beast, the one whom we call "the Antichrist".

There is yet one more picture, one of "the great harlot" (ch.17) riding on this composite beast, and considerable detail is given concerning this harlot, who is identified with Babylon (v. 5). This harlot must represent the monetary or economic system, while the beast stands for the political or governmental ruling agency, the composite of all the governments of the image and the beasts of Daniel.

If this all seems a little confusing, take heart! Daniel's visions and prophecies, and the prophecies of John in the Revelation are all one and the same! The image, the beasts, the two animals, the composite beast, and the harlot, are <u>*all* one and the same thing!</u> The five kingdoms represented by the image and the beasts in Daniel all came and went as kingdoms (except, of course, the final one), but are yet existing in their "extension" of life in another form so that they can all be destroyed together at the same time in "*the time of the end*". Though these individual kingdoms no longer exist, nor are they of any consequence in this time of the end, they are all united into one entity, a composite

111

amalgamation as a world-ruling, world-dom-
inating, controlling power in the final days of
time. Out of this composite amalgamation come
"the Antichrist" and the false prophet, as well as
all that is prophesied concerning the final hours
of man on the earth.

Daniel 7:12 gives clear evidence of this,
where the angel speaking with Daniel declares
that the *"dominion" of the beasts (kingdoms) will
be taken away, but "…an extension of life…"* will
be granted to them for an *appointed period of
time*! Though they have no dominion or kingdom
for the time of this extension of life, they continue
to exist with influence until the time appointed
for their destruction (v. 13 & 14) when God's
kingdom will be established by His Son, and
"the saints of the Most High".

In all of this we have stopped short of taking
a look at the final unnamed kingdom which is
represented by the ten horns of the beast, and
the feet and ten toes of the image.

112

It seems to be nearly universally proclaimed that these "ten" represent a revived Roman Empire, which is said to be resident in the current "European Common Market", or "European Union". On the surface this appears to be feasible, even possibly likely. Let me remind you at this point, however, that this idea is merely a "theory", an interpretation and opinion, not necessarily a revelation of truth. Any disagreement with this interpretation does not constitute heresy. Remember the Urim and Thummim - the Oracle.

Consider some thoughts concerning this matter. This attempt to equate this final kingdom with the European Union is primarily based on the old geographical boundaries of the Roman Empire. It is assumed that because all of the Common Market nations lie basically within these boundaries, this must be the fulfillment of this part of the prophecy.

This fails to take into account some rather clear factors of Scripture, and leaves several very important, pertinent questions unanswered.

113

First, if Babylon, Medo-Persia, and Greece, though very much a part of the prophecy of this end time, are not equated in any way with the geographical location they previously occupied, how can we do it with Rome? Secondly, if the boundaries of the ancient Roman Empire were traced on a current map, we could count all or part of at least twenty countries (possibly more), not just ten! As of the break-up of the Soviet Union, there are now well over twenty nations that are members of the European Union, and several more making application and very likely to be accepted in the next few years. The number 'ten' is now moot, and will be completely insignificant when all of this is finally accomplished! (As of this printing there are 27 nations in the EU.)

Finally, and probably most significant, according to the prophecies of Daniel, **all** of the kingdoms in Daniel's prophecies are to be understood as *world-ruling, world-controlling powers*! Each previous kingdom held clear dominion over the entire known civilized world of their time.

114

They were economically, politically, and militarily dominant. This final kingdom, in order to fit the prophetic picture, must have clear dominance and control over the rest of the world. As of the present, and in the foreseeable future, the European Union is, at best, a third or fourth-rate power in the world! It displays no promise or projection of *ever* being anything more! In order for them to rise to that necessary place of dominance in *all* areas of influence, the USA, Russia, possibly China and even Japan, would have to lose or relinquish *all* of their current influence or current power. All of these nations combined do not wield the power and influence through out the whole world as does the United States of America! In <u>all</u> areas - economics, technology, education, military, political, etc. - *nobody* comes close to wielding the power and influence of this nation, and as we watch, that influence is getting greater and greater, not less and less. This final kingdom cannot be anything *but* the USA today, if

Really?

why?

Not so

115

we really believe that our time is short and we are actually living in the very last days of time.

It appears, therefore, that the entirety of the image, which would necessarily include the feet and toes, and its correlation with the beasts in their composite form and all that they represent, is identifiable with but one nation in these final days of time - the mightiest, most influential of all nations in the history of the world! If this is true, then it must follow that the "Antichrist" and his false prophet <u>will</u> in fact, rise up out of <u>this</u> very nation, and not from some other far removed place on the globe.

No!
Daniel
9:26,27

Now, if all of this *is* valid, it becomes all the more clear how easily so many people will be fooled - deceived - by an "antichrist" and false prophet arising from right here among us. Even as those scholars of two millenniums ago argued that no prophet would arise out of Galilee, or Nazareth, and thus missed their Messiah when He came to them, even so, it may very well be that while thousands, even millions, are carefully

116

watching for this "antichrist" under certain pre-determined, perceived conditions due to human interpretation, they could just find themselves very easily following and supporting the very one they have been fearing.

The political leaders of this great nation are not 'kings" in the sense of those mentioned in the prophecies, but are leaders or rulers who are elected by the people they rule. The Antichrist will come to power, most likely, by the current prevailing political process at the time. He will not be able to win an election in this country without fooling a pretty large majority of professing Christians. It is highly likely that a whole lot of good Christian people may actually end up voting into office the very one who will prove to be the "Antichrist".

* At this time it is essential to insert something of great importance. The initial evidence which prompted the writing of this document was received sometime in 1974. The original manuscript was completed within about a year

117

after that. The manuscript has been updated a couple of times since then to insert some pieces of new information received over the years since, but nothing has been received to change the premises or conclusions in any way. For example, the break-up of the Soviet Union and the Communistic rule in those countries occurred well after the initial manuscript, but played a role in supporting the information already included in the document. Therefore, the document required an updating to include that information.

Some may notice in close consideration of the original writings of this document that any attempt to specifically identify the ten horns and ten toes has been avoided. With the identification of the image and the beasts being determined to be the United States of America, it has been properly assumed that the ten toes and ten horns must, of necessity, be identified with the same entity. But it has been a terribly elusive thing to be more specific! What could

118

there be in this entity that would be identified with the number "ten", and would be identifiable as "kingdoms", with rulers? This has admittedly stymied the author for over fifteen years, while continuing to pray and wait for an answer. Along with *this* sought for answer, one was needed, also, for the seven heads of the composite beast of Revelation. That, too, proved to be elusive.

Something came into my possession that helps clarify the whole picture, and has helped to identity these more specifically. I suppose the Lord knew that this would need to be clarified before the document, which has been held in a file for these years, could be published and disseminated! Consequently, He withheld this vital information until an appropriate time, according to His timing and infinite wisdom.

A book was published in 1992, which uncovered and detailed the plans and engineering of the so-called "New World Order", or unified world government. It was a book entitled, "En Route to Global Occupation", and was authored by

119

Gary H. Kah, who had been a high ranking government liaison during the 1980's, and worked as an insider under the administrations of both Presidents Reagan and Bush 1. He investigated into and uncovered some vital information of the plans and operations of this element, and, as a Christian, felt obligated to publish the information. I highly recommend that all believers get their hands on this book and read it carefully. It contains some astonishing revelations, but probably the most astonishing to this author was the very glaring and clear picture which completed the puzzle of the image and the beasts of these prophetic visions!

The political and social engineers of the New World Order have divided the entire world into ten regions which they had initially called "kingdoms", with each projected to have their own "king", or ruler who rules under the authority of the one supreme ruler of the whole plan, with the headquarters located in New York City! That one may well be one of the ten. As I study the map which was reprinted in this book from the original, it shows that region one includes what is now the USA and Canada and has since been expanded to include Mexico, hence all of North America, while region two is all of western Europe, and region three is Japan. This would indicate that the center of this whole system will be in the region designated as region one. This system was first devised and its recommendations published, though only for select eyes, certainly not for the public, in 1973! That was just about one year, at the most, before this picture of the image and the beasts was made clear to this writer, and the seal on the prophecies of Daniel was broken. Even to this writer that is rather chilling.

This system was the product of a self-appointed committee which called itself "The Club of Rome", under the "authority" of the New World Order Planners. The author of this book, Mr. Kah, makes note that in his determination, "Most of the directives for the planning of the world government are coming from the Club of Rome." He also notes that "the club's findings and recommendations are published from time to time in special, highly confidential reports, which are sent to the power elite to be implemented. On 17 September 1973 the Club released one such report, entitled *Regionalized and Adaptive Model of the Global World System...*" this report having been prepared by two of the members of the Club of Rome.

Mr. Kah goes on from there to report that "The document reveals that the club has divided the world into ***ten political/economic regions, which it refers to as 'kingdoms'.*** (This sounds to me like a fulfillment of Daniel 7:15-28 and Revelation 13 in the making.)" What a perfect picture of the ten toes and ten horns, which are, in fact, emanating from the central operating point of the system in the USA, but are blanketing the whole earth making this a rather clear fulfillment of the prophetic picture.

There is one more quote from this book which I wish to include before returning to my original text. Mr. Kah observes, "Having gained some idea of America's role in building the New World Order, the only remaining question I had was, 'what will happen to the U.S. once it has fulfilled its mission?'" He goes on further to observe, "As things currently stand, New York would be the logical choice to be the world's capitol, given the fact that it is the most powerful and influential city in the world and that the United Nations, the Council on Foreign Relations, and the Trilateral Commission are all headquartered there. However, the secret hierarchy of Europe, which is still ultimately in charge, might have different plans. If they intend to locate the world capitol in Europe, they will find a way to do so. Such a decision, however, would probably involve either the economic devastation or physical destruction of New York City. This could be accomplished in several ways - economically, through a planned collapse of the stock market or

123

a severe depression resulting from our national debt; or physically, as an act of terrorism, as a nuclear "accident", or through a limited nuclear war. Whatever method would be selected, the European Hierarchy, I believe, would be capable of carrying it out (if God allows)."

(Is it possible that the attack on the World Trade Center was an attempt to accomplish this? But since it would violate the prophetic picture that God has given us, He saw to it that any effort to utterly destroy New York City would not be successful, and its recovery would be virtually complete and successful.)

He goes on to say in the next paragraph, "Is New York destined for destruction? I don't know the answer to this question, nor do I wish such a fate upon the people of that city. However, the parallels between New York and the great, but wicked, city described as Mystery Babylon in Revelation 17 and 18 are difficult to ignore. *__I can only hope these passages are describing something else!__*" (Emphasis mine.)

124

I will resist the temptation to go further with this picture except to comment that the seven heads of the beast of Revelation, in the light of the identity of the horns, can only be understood as the seven continents which the ten horns cover and fill. I cannot see at this point how it can be understand it in any other way.

Before bringing this entire matter to a conclusion, there is one further area or direction of thinking that should be considered. Over the generations of time, multitudes of preachers and writers have made many attempts to unravel the mysteries surrounding the second coming of Christ, particularly the identity of the "Antichrist" and the false prophet, and the secret of the "mark of the beast", the number 666. The speculations and theories have run rampant over the years. Within my own generation there have been an abundance of suspects, including such ones as Hitler, Mussolini, the Pope, Stalin, and even Henry Kissinger.

There are a few things which we know about these two which may well take care of the whole list. The Bible makes some very plain and clear statements, but apparently some of these statements have been interpreted, over-looked, added-to, or taken away from. First, this "Antichrist" is never called "the Antichrist" in the Bible. (This is the reason we have usually used quote marks whenever we have used the word.) Secondly, an examination of all the statements in the bible concerning the Beast will point up some rather glaring omissions in most previous approaches to the matter. Both the Beast and the false prophet are described as religious, moral believers in supernatural manifestations of power, "miracles, signs and wonders", etc. They present to the world a formula for peace and a philosophy or policy for "getting along" which becomes very popular and acceptable to the vast majority of the populations of the world. Their presentation of themselves and their phi-losophies is so idealistically good, that Jesus said that even "...**the very elect**..." would be deceived if it were possible to deceive them! That can *only* be understood as something or someone which will be appealing even to "the very elect" - Christians, church people, even evangelicals and conservatives. They will not be repulsed by them! Not one of the men previously named, or any others on the seemingly endless list, can even be said to come close to this picture.

I won't presume to try to identify this duo, as so many have, but maybe I can present a series of evidences which will help to make them more easily identified and recognized when they <u>do</u> come to power. Remembering the cases of Simeon and Anna and the small minority of people who actually recognized Christ and the kind of people who were in that select group, as well as the principle of the Urim and Thummim, I do approach this with great caution! The actual ability to identify these men readily will not rest with mere, simple knowledge about them even

127

from the Scriptures, but will rest fully upon each individual's ability to access in complete humility the working of the New Testament Oracle - the Lights and Perfections - which God makes available.

This Beast will have as a close advisor and helper one who is called the false prophet. Many consider a false prophet to be anyone who teaches something which is of a religious nature which is false, or anyone who pretends to be a spokesman for God but speaks error. Both Jesus and Paul made distinctions between false "prophets", false "apostles", false "teachers", and false "ministers of righteousness". In other words, not everyone who teaches or preaches something false or falsely represents themselves as representatives of God is in the category of a false "prophet". According to God's own definition, a false prophet is one who claims or is acclaimed to be a prophet, or to speak prophetic utterances, claiming direct prophetic authority from God, but who actually speaks from his own

inspiration or the inspiration of the great imper-
sonator of God, Satan himself! A false prophet is
also one who speaks a prophetic word, claiming
it to be from God, and that word does not come
to pass. There are not a great many men today
who would fall into that category, especially
among those who would be in a place of promi-
nence sufficient to be or become a close asso-
ciate and advisor to a world political leader, or
who would be in the category of one who could
deceive even the very elect! In fact, there are
not many today who even acknowledge the
existence of prophets.

Since it appears we are talking about <u>this</u>
nation, and since we are concerned with a professed prophet, what do we know of and have
here in this country which could even possibly
fit this picture? I think we can exclude off the top
all minor cults and their alleged "prophets" or
"messiahs", because they represent no power
or ability sufficient to deceive <u>any</u> of the genuine
"very elect". No Jim Jones type, or Sun Myong

129

Moon, or Elizabeth Claire Prophet can impress enough people of "the very elect" to pose much of a danger. Remember that those who are "the very elect" will not necessarily be *actually* deceived, but the deception will be so remarkable that they could be deceived if it were possible to deceive them. Don't forget, also, that this 'false prophet' produces miracles which the Bible describes as "lying signs and wonders" (II Thess. 2:8-10), which even includes calling down fire from heaven (Rev. 13:13)! (Stay alert, though, because the "Two Witnesses" are said to do something very similar to this, too!) People of the kind which we have named are not producing anything in the way of "…great signs and wonders", and most don't even profess to do so, to the best of my knowledge. We should also consider who those might be of whom Jesus said they would come to Him *"…in that day…"* and protest, *"…Lord! Lord! Have we not done many wonderful works [including casting out devils] **in thy name?**"*(Matt. 7:22-23) Might we

130

not be very likely looking at the prospects that we will be dealing with someone who actually calls Jesus *"Lord",* and uses His name in the casting out of devils and in the performing all those many wonderful works?!! This possibility, or **probability**, continues to limit the field of possible identities!

Who, then, do we know of in this nation of ours who 1) are religious, even probably claiming or professing to be "Christian"; 2) acknowledge and claim the existence of a prophet; and 3) believe in and practice the working of miracles, or "signs and wonders"?

To the best of my knowledge there are only three religious groups in this country, maybe in the whole world, who fit all three of these criteria; the old-line Pentecostals, the neo-Pentecostals or contemporary Charismatics, and the Mormons. It may not be commonly known, but the Mormon Church claims to believe in and practice a "baptism of the Holy Spirit" and speaking in tongues, and they profess to practice spiritual gifts, including healing by the laying on of hands, and *the working of miracles*! They also claim to be doing it in the name of Jesus Christ! After all, they are "The Church of Jesus Christ of Latter Day Saints". It is mostly common knowledge, however that they do believe in the existence of prophets for this age, although they acknowledge only one at a time, and that being the man who sits as their president, presiding over the church. As of the time of the original writing of this manuscript, quite interestingly, that man happened to be Ezra Taft Benson, a man who had been most active in our government, having been appointed to serve as Secretary of Agriculture under President Eisenhower! (As of the re-typing and updating of this treatise, Benson has died, and a new president has been selected for the Mormon Church, and the current president is Thomas Monson.)

I believe it is readily and easily seen that the old-line Pentecostals have no serious political ambitions, especially on a world-wide scope, but even within this country. The neo-Pentecostals, or Charismatics, seem to have developed somewhat of a move in the direction of political involvement, but it does not appear as yet that they have any kind of major influence in the total political spectrum. Most of their activities in this field are, at present, only in the category of grass roots political activism, not in the wielding of much actual political clout in the decision making chambers. However, considering some of the startling information in Mr. Kah's book it may be conceivable that something like that could possibly occur in fairly short order. They may have the ability to put pressure on the government, and influence much of its operation, but they are definitely not in the ranks of the power brokers or decision makers, and certainly wield little significant influence there.

However, the Mormons do have serious political ambitions, and they also actually believe and preach and teach, and overtly *practice their believing,* that they are destined to be *"God's*

Kingdom on the Earth". They are firmly convinced that their destiny is to rule the world. In practicing it, they have made unbelievable inroads into the total governing structure of our society at every level. From local governments, school boards, county governments, state governments, to the federal government, they have made their way into prominent, influential, even controlling positions all the way along. Many of the agencies of the government are under their complete control at the present time, including, of course, the Department of Agriculture, where Ezra Taft Benson set the course while in that cabinet position, having been appointed by President Eisenhower. He proceeded to appoint to high positions in the various forests of the Forest Service and all departments under the oversight of the Department of Agriculture, Mormons wherever one could be found to fill those positions. In virtually all branches of the Agriculture Department there is now a Mormon in charge.

In practically <u>all</u> areas of Social Welfare and in control of the Child Protective Services the Mormons have taken virtual complete control as a result of George Romney having been appointed by President Richard Nixon to the Cabinet position which regulates these areas of government control. Mr. Romney, like Benson before him, was one of the Council of Twelve Apostles of the Mormon Church for quite a number of years. There is a very disproportionately high percentage of Mormons in both houses of Congress at the present time, some of whom are secret members.

Now, as this book is preparing for publication, George Romney's son, Mitt, is a strong candidate for the Republican nomination for the office of President of the United States. As we continue to evaluate the Scriptural declarations concerning the things we are considering here, that may well become a matter of a greater cause for concern.

On top of this, I have seen documentation both in writing and through TV journalism that the top recruiting ground for the FBI and the CIA is Brigham Young University in Utah, the Mormon College.

(It would also be well to note here, without going into detail, that there is a strong bond and tie between the Mormon Church and the secret society of Freemasons, or the Masonic Lodge, with their New Age connection.)

All of this would not really be quite so alarming if it were not for the fact that they so closely fit the description of the Beast and the False Prophet of the end times, and if they did not so openly, even blatantly, declare themselves as aspiring to complete political control. Several years ago I saw a book published by the Mormons through their Deseret Publishing Company in Salt Lake City entitled "God's Kingdom on the Earth" which detailed their strong conviction that this is their destiny, to rule the world. After all, they are fine, moral, high-standards type people, and we "conservatives" should be delighted to have so many such people in all these places of government, should we not? If I understand the Word properly, isn't this **precisely** the manner in which the Beast and False Prophet are going to attempt to deceive "...*even the very elect...*"? Even more disturbing is the fact that at this point of time there are *many* Christians, Evangelicals, Fundamentalists, and Charismatics included, who have become softened in their attitudes toward them, and have found themselves walking hand in hand with them in all of the "conservative" causes, "bedfellows", if you will, in virtually all moral, social, and political issues. They are blinded to any potential danger. Even some of the national leaders in the Fundamental Christian political and social activism circles have come out publicly endorsing and supporting Mormons for high political office simply because they are talking the same language, and are espousing the same moral positions which we as true Christians hold. It has been a point of alarm for me to see how many of our top Evangelical leaders have jumped on the bandwagon of the candidacy of Mitt Romney for president. There has obviously not been a very deep examination into the Mormon background and their determination to rule the world, and their strategies and tactics by which they intend to accomplish that.

I am not prepared as yet to suggest or make any kind of declaration concerning the actual identity of the Beast (Antichrist) and the False Prophet, but what we are watching develop right under our noses is at the very least a potential scenario for those prophetic figures to sneak into power and become the rulers of the world with all approval and support of even a large part of contemporary Christian leaders. Whether Mitt Romney is destined to step into the role of the Antichrist is still something to be revealed, but the position he is in as a candidate at this time, and with his essential devotion to all that Mormonism requires concerning their "prophet" president, the possibility is something to be considered and watch for.

Even if this is not the case, might we not be being conditioned and prepared to support the very man who, by strong deception, will come to power as described in the words of prophecy? Will we, as professing Christians, in the absence of the "Oracle", actually <u>help</u> bring to power with our full support, even possibly our votes, whoever is to become the Antichrist? Is this not similar, in reverse, to the very unfolding of events in the time of Christ?

One very notable and high profile leader in the Fundamental, Conservative arm of Christianity, who has been very active in the social and political arena of our day, said not very long ago in my hearing, that he could and would support and encourage <u>any</u> man for high public office, even and especially for president, who publically stood for the high moral principles which we as Christians hold and espouse, whether he was a "born again Christian" nor not. He was responding to charges that he and others with him wanted only "born again Christians" in office,

139

and were trying to take over the government in that way. He specifically stated that his support would include people from other faiths, such as Catholic, or Jewish, or ***Mormon!*** (emphasis mine!). We are obviously seeing an uncomfortably large number and percentage of our current "spiritual leaders" - the Scribes (Bible scholars), and the Pharisees (the traditionalists or conservatives), and the Sadducees (the liberals), and even the Priests (pastors and preachers and evangelists, etc.) - moving toward acceptance of the Mormons into the spectrum of acceptability as a religious body, most especially for social and political purposes, which is actually playing right into their hands. Might not this lead to these very leaders becoming the very fulfillment of the prophecies which they are so knowledgeable about, just like those of their counterparts in Christ's day?

With just such an attitude among millions of professing Christians, how utterly simple, and with what unbelievable ease, will this "Antichrist" and his False Prophet slip into power, under the radar, unawares and undetected, with the initial full support and approval of a majority of those who make a profession of Jesus as Lord! It matters not whether they consider themselves Charismatics, or Fundamentalists, or Evangelicals, or Conservatives, or Liberals, or whatever! If even *"the very elect"* would be deceived if it were possible, what of those who are pretenders to the title, who are backslidden in heart, and who are among those of Laodicea who believe and profess themselves to be spiritually *"rich and increased in goods..."*, etc., but are oblivious to the fact that they are utterly departed from the faith once delivered to the saints? The deception will be thorough and complete where these are concerned, until it is too late to do anything about it! Those in Christ's day who were so Biblically knowledgeable were fooled. How much more certain and tragic will be the deception of their counterparts in our day by *"the angel of light"*, the personification of Lucifer, "the light

141

bearer", himself, and his false *"ministers of righteousness"* in the sad absence of the Oracle!

We must, therefore, conclude that it is not, nor can it be, superior scholarship, or simple sound doctrine alone, or correct theology, nor acceptance and recognition by our peers or the masses, which will assure us the means of discerning the Messiah or his antithetical counterpart, the "antichrist". The Urim and Thummim of this era is not just for the scholars, or the spiritual elite, whoever they are. It is available to each and every individual believer, no matter his degree of knowledge of the Word. The understanding of the knowledge which we **do** have is ours by means of this Oracle right now. It is available for anyone for the obtaining of the necessary knowledge and understanding, and recognition of the *"...things to come"*, which Jesus also said was a part of the ministry and work of the Holy Ghost. This *manifest Presence of God* in the Oracle, New Testament version, is certainly available to any and all who will humble themselves before

God in boldness, yet with a contrite heart until He responds, and those "stones" light up assuring His presence and assistance in this situation. None should ever allow themselves to be content or satisfied until the Spirit of God responds and causes His Personal Presence to be made known unquestionably. Then, and *only* then, can there be a positive assurance of that Urim and Thummim working to bring the recognition of the events and the people involved when the time comes, and that time is very, **very** close at hand! I cannot help but believe that this is the only means by which "the very elect" can be protected from the deception.

Never forget, **Jesus said it,** ***"If any man will do His will he shall know of the doctrine [teaching] whether it be of God, or whether I speak of Myself!"*** **(John 7:17).**

ADENDUM (EPILOG?)

How I came to
write this paper

My Mom told me that when I was just a little boy I was the most inquisitive kid she had ever seen. I wanted to know everything about everything! I wanted to know how every little mechanical thing worked. I even found a way to take some of my toys apart to examine the various parts so I could figure out how they worked. Unfortunately, I wasn't able to reassemble most of them. I drove Mom to distraction by the incessant barrage of questions about almost anything and everything that crossed my mind.

As I grew, my inquisitiveness grew with me, and even today I must admit that I am still just a very inquisitive little boy in a grown man's body. My love for God and all that He represents has been deep and strong. I have sought diligently and long to get a handle on whatever I read in the Bible, and have spent much time in study and examination. As questions would arise in my mind while reading and studying, I would devote myself to the pursuit of a satisfying answer.

One day in the early 1970's I was challenged with a mystery. I had been inspired by something Jesus said, recorded in Matthew 13 in between the parable of "the sower" and the explanation of that parable for His disciples. When they asked Him why He continually spoke to the people in parables, He answered, *"To you it has been given to know the mysteries of the kingdom of God, but to them it has not been given."* I spent some time musing on those words, and was quite intent on finding out what He might have meant.

So I was led to the second chapter of the book of Daniel where Nebuchadnezzar had a dream and couldn't remember it, even though it troubled him greatly. He called all of his "wise" men, the *"...magicians, the astrologers, the sorcerers, and the Chaldeans..."* and demanded that they tell him what he had dreamed, then tell him the meaning or interpretation of it. When they could not do this, he lost all patience with them and ordered that they should be executed. When Daniel heard of this, he requested to see the king with the promise of meeting the king's demands.

After spending time in prayer and getting his associates to pray, he went before the king and declared the very thing he wanted by telling him what he had dreamed, then telling him the interpretation. You have read about this already, so I will not repeat any of it here. The challenge was presented to me to pursue and find out what had become of the kingdoms represented by the gold and silver and bronze and iron throughout the rest of time until now, bringing them to the time

147

of the end when the stone would hit the image in its feet and crush it all together at the same time. Where are the remnants of those four kingdoms or empires today? That became my challenge, and I became almost obsessed with that pursuit.

I had once written a paper about this image and the beasts and all that they represented when I was in Bible College for my class on Old Testament Survey. But I had not seen any of these implications in this scenario that all of these kingdoms would be given an *"...extension of life..."* until the time of the end, so I never even thought before this to examine into it. So I was challenged to search out and find the solution to this mystery.

I took the challenge seriously, and I went into it with full intent of devoting all the time and effort necessary to discover the solution, and identify each of those entities. I went through numerous books and commentaries searching for some evidence that would lead to a valid conclusion. I sought out books on the subject in hopes of picking up some clue. I devoted myself and my time, apart from my necessary work to make a living and take care of my family. For more than two full years I searched and probed and prayed and struggled to learn all I could about the subject, but nothing came together for me. Few other things got through into my mind during that span of time, and I felt almost driven to finding the solution. Although I didn't keep count, I probably read through these passages in Daniel many times, maybe as many as 20 or more, but all to no avail. Oh, I certainly did learn a lot, but the actual understanding eluded me completely. I was frustrated and yet unshaken in my determination. I remained determined to find the answer one way or another, even if I had to keep searching for the rest of my life.

After something over two years of intense searching and coming up empty, I was reading again one day in the final chapter, chapter 12, of Daniel, and as I was reading it again, for the umpteenth time, I saw that the angel spoke to

Daniel and said, *"But you, Daniel, <u>shut up the words, and seal the book until the time of the end</u>; many shall run to and fro, and knowledge shall increase."* Then as I read a little further I saw this again, *"And he said, "Go your way, Daniel, <u>for the words are closed up and sealed till the time of the end</u>. Many shall be purified, made white, and refined, but the wicked shall do wickedly; and none of the wicked shall understand, but the wise shall understand."* That's when it hit me! For more than two full years I had been trying to get into something that God had sealed and He had not opened the seal yet for anyone. I had been probing into something that was not available for human investigation. As long as the seal was in place it could not be tapped until the time of the end when God, Himself, would break the seal and give understanding.

So I closed my notebook and set it aside and determined to pursue no more until I could see some evidence that the seal had been broken. I began to keep a watchful eye on prophecy to know what was being learned so I could be aware as soon as possible of the breaking of the seal. I didn't even think any more about the issue that had been forefront in my mind for the previous two years, except that when it would pass through my mind, I would breathe a prayer that God would open the seal soon.

At that time I was pastor of a church in central California, and my four children were still pretty young. It was in the mid-70's, and I was scheduled to attend a pastor's meeting in Southern California, so we had someone come and watch our children, and my wife and I drove south for the meeting, which, as I recall, lasted for about three days. It wasn't particularly notable, but I always have enjoyed the fellowship and interaction with my fellow pastors. As we were on the drive home, traveling up highway 99 through California, I was reflecting on the subject matter of the meeting, and was meditating before the Lord about some things. Far removed from my mind was any thought of the Daniel's prophecies.

151

There were some songs and choruses that I was humming as I pondered the matters of the previous few days, and my wife had fallen asleep in the passenger seat next to me.

I suddenly became aware, or thought it was an awareness, of another Presence in the car. It was an overwhelming sense of another Presence. I glanced in the rear view mirror to check the back seat, and then glanced over my shoulder just to be sure. Then, without any warning of any kind, suddenly my mind jumped to the issues of the prophecies in Daniel, and in a very brief moment of time the identity of all of the parts of the image and all of the beasts of Daniel's vision that came to him much later in his life, came into my mind. It all came together in a perfect blending of historical and contemporary identities and it all fit perfectly with the presentation. My flesh tingled and my heart raced and I had to catch my breath! I almost had to pull over to the side of the highway and stop, but instead just lifted my foot from the accelerator and continued driving, feeling almost like I had lifted a few inches from the seat of the car.

My wife was still sleeping to my right, and I could hardly keep myself from waking her and telling her what had just happened. It far exceeded my most intense desire and dream, and I thought, "Is it possible the seal had just been broken?" That thought virtually took my breath away for a few moments. It still has that same effect on me.

In just a matter of a few minutes that seemed like an eternity, my wife awoke and stretched, and I said to her, "Honey, you won't believe what just happened!!" I told her what had occurred, and she just calmly said something like, "Oh that's nice."

When we arrived at home and settled back into the parsonage, I sat down and began to check some things out and found that the whole picture actually did fit perfectly, and what I have written here, with some insertions along the way, is the result of that brief few minutes on highway

99 just a few miles south of Bakersfield. I sincerely hope and pray that the significance of this will touch your heart and bless your soul as it has mine while I have waited for the time and opportunity to publish it. I have been encouraged several times over the years by various people I have shared it with to get it published. One such was a man who lived near us in California that I shared it with not long after the incident. He was a man with a Doctorate in Bible and Theology and also in psychology, and was the psychologist for a neighboring school district not far from us. There have been a few others since then, the most recent being a friend who was owner and manager of a Christian Bookstore for many years, and was well versed in Biblical matters on this general topic. He had closed his store and moved to another part of the country to pursue other avenues of service. I sent him this writing, and he called me and urged me strongly to seek to get it published. It was this latest encouragement that triggered the decision to now seek

publication. I hope and pray and trust this book will bless your heart and open it up to the voice of God's Holy Spirit as you pursue the truth in this and all things.

GF

CPSIA information can be obtained at www.ICGtesting.com
Printed in the USA
BVOW070112230712

295811BV00001B/1/P